Karen H Thompson

The Lace Samples from Ipswich, Massachusetts, 1789-1790

History, Patterns, and Working Diagrams for 22 Lace Samples Preserved at the Library of Congress

ISBN 978-0-9990385-0-5

Copyright © Karen H Thompson 2017

1st edition

Photos by author except where noted

Contents

- 4   Foreword
- 5   Acknowledgements
- 6   Original samples from 1789-1790
- 7   Introduction
- 14   Images of original samples
- 15   Images of reconstructed samples
- 16   Technical Information about the Lace Samples and Making the Lace
- 20   Working Diagrams
- 21   Overview of dimensions and common elements of original lace samples

Patterns and Working Diagrams organized by style:

- 44   Ipswich Sample 1
- 24   Ipswich Sample 2
- 50   Ipswich Sample 3
- 56   Ipswich Sample 4
- 32   Ipswich Sample 5
- 46   Ipswich Sample 6
- 26   Ipswich Sample 7
- 28   Ipswich Sample 8
- 52   Ipswich Sample 9
- 54   Ipswich Sample 10
- 30   Ipswich Sample 11
- 62   Ipswich Sample 12
- 48   Ipswich Sample 13
- 60   Ipswich Sample 14
- 58   Ipswich Sample 15
- 64   Ipswich Sample 16
- 38   Ipswich Sample 17
- 36   Ipswich Sample 18
- 40   Ipswich Sample 19
- 42   Ipswich Sample 19 detailed diagrams
- 34   Ipswich Sample 20
- 66   Ipswich Sample 21
- 68   Ipswich Sample 22
- 70   Ipswich Sample 22 detailed diagrams

- 72   Biography

Foreword

Held within the Textiles collection at the National Museum of American History is an extraordinary collection of hand- and machine-made lace, donated by generous collectors over the course of a century or more. The collection spans much of the history of lace, from the 16th century into the 20th. And for more than a decade, Karen Thompson has been that collection's advocate, ensuring that object records and images are available to online visitors, writing blog posts about our amazing objects, and guiding a monthly program of lacemaking demonstrations for visitors to NMAH.

This book on the laces of Ipswich, Massachusetts, is the result of many years of Karen's studying and teaching lacemaking. In this volume, she has given us the tools to recreate one of the United States' first industries – a cottage industry – but an industry nonetheless. Making lace by hand is now, for the most part, a leisure time activity. These working diagrams of the Ipswich samples will allow enthusiasts to recreate the laces, but in addition, they give those who don't make lace a window into the world of Hamiltonian Ipswich – a town that relied on 600 women lacemakers for a substantial portion of its income, for a product that connected it to the rest of the country. The samples and the patterns testify to the skills and business acumen those women possessed, and to the struggles for economic independence they endured. Perhaps these fragile remnants of their work, collected for Alexander Hamilton's review of the American economy, will inspire the next hit Broadway musical.

Madelyn Shaw
Curator of Textiles
National Museum of American History
Smithsonian Institution
Washington, DC

I am honored to be asked by Karen H. Thompson to comment on her authoritative book, The Lace Samples from Ipswich, Massachusetts, 1789-1790.

As a lace maker, I can say with certainty that Karen has produced the definitive text on American Ipswich lace. Working for years to reconstruct the samples of Ipswich Lace held at the Library of Congress in Washington, DC, she has brought from the shores of England to the shores of early America the story of a unique lace that is now, via her book, firmly placed in historic and present context.
It has been my pleasure to volunteer with Karen Thompson at the Smithsonian Museum of American History, where she has given our country many years of dedicated service.

Her book is a thoughtful and intellectual text that elevates Ipswich Lace to its rightful place in American history. What makes the book endearing is that it is also a reflection of a thoughtful and intellectual author and lace maker.

I congratulate Karen and sincerely wish her much success with her book.

Joyce Arsnow
Silver Spring, Maryland

Acknowledgements

This book would not have become a reality without the help and input of numerous people. I am extremely grateful to all who have contributed in one way or another.
The biggest tribute goes to the lace makers in Ipswich, Massachusetts, who created this beautiful lace in the late 1700s. Then to my late mother, who taught me to make and love bobbin lace. To Marta Cotterell for introducing me and other members of the Chesapeake Region Lace Guild to the Ipswich laces at a lace get-together at Tamara Webb's house in the 1990s, and to Sheryl de Jong, who came along to the Library of Congress on numerous occasions to start drafting patterns for the Ipswich lace samples and was my partner in trying them out and sharing what we had found.

The staff at the Reading Room at the Library of Congress have been very helpful and curious about this endeavor. During a number years of teaching workshops on Ipswich lace, I am grateful to my students who have been willing to try making this late 18th century American lace. The mistakes they have found and suggestions they have given me on the patterns or working diagrams have helped improve them. I appreciate the encouragement from fellow lace makers in pursuing my dream of making this lace available to others, and for help and suggestions on early drafts of the manuscript. Thanks go to fellow lace makers Gil Dye, Jean Leader, Kim Davis, Louise Colgan, Mary Tod, and Joyce Arsnow, who, among others, have taken time away from their own projects and busy lives to give advice on this book. My sincere thanks also go to our daughter, Kristina, for her edits and suggestions, and to our grandchildren for their willingness to make bobbin lace with their grandmother.

My gratitude extends to my supervisor, Madelyn Shaw, Curator of Textiles at the Smithsonian American History Museum in Washington, DC, for her encouragement and help. Julie Miller, Early American Historian at the Library of Congress, and Katherine Chaison, Curator of Ipswich Museum in Ipswich, MA, have both added useful historical details. I am also grateful to Bev Wolov, fellow Smithsonian volunteer and photographer, who captured some of the images used.

Last, but not least, I could not have spent so many hours on this project without the full support of my entire family, and especially of my husband, Bob, who is fascinated by the mechanics of bobbin lace. His red pen has been put to good use on many early drafts. I am very appreciative for all his support.

Washington, DC, in the spring of 2017
Karen H. Thompson

The original samples from Ipswich made between August 1789 and August 1790.

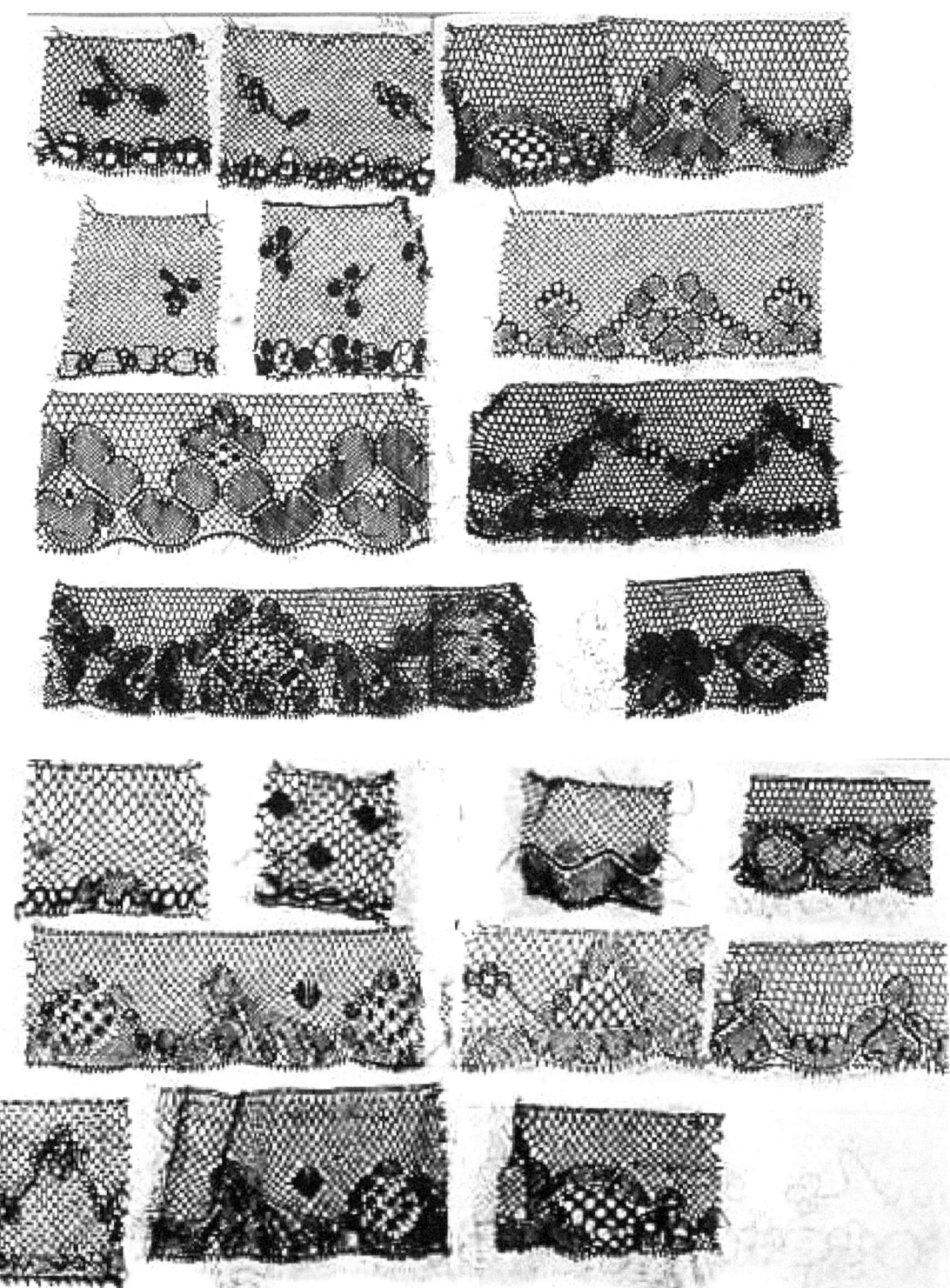

Samples mounted on two sheets of paper before the current mount on acid-free board. (Courtesy the Library of Congress)

Introduction

The Library of Congress, in Washington, DC, has a rare collection of 21 black silk bobbin lace samples made in Ipswich, Massachusetts, between 1789 and 1790. The samples have been stored with Alexander Hamilton's papers since 1791 and are now in the Manuscript Division of the Library of Congress, where I was able to study them in detail before making reproductions.

Why are they there? After the first US Congress convened (New York, 1789), one of its earliest acts was to task Alexander Hamilton, the country's first Secretary of the Treasury, with taking a census of manufacturing in the 13 original states. Included in the information gathered was a report from Ipswich, Massachusetts, on the town's handmade lacemaking industry.[1] This request was conveyed through Mr. George Cabot, a wealthy merchant from Salem, MA, and a US senator from June 1791 to 1796, who, in turn, asked the Reverend Joseph Dana to collect this information from, in, and around Ipswich.

Mr. Dana surveyed the Ipswich households and found that there were two kinds of manufacturing, both related to textiles. One was cordage (rope) and the other, lace. On lace, Mr. Dana reported that, in the town of Ipswich, there were *"probably not less than 600 persons who do more or less in it; some devoting the most of their time to; others, little intervals only: some employed in the smaller patterns, others in the larger and more complex; and all independent of each other..."*[2] Further, Mr. Dana wrote (Jan 24, 1791) that *"in various parts of Mass^{ts} the Females make Lace & edging for their own use & some small parcels for sale – but I believe the manufacture has nowhere become of sufficient consequence to attract notice except at Ipswich..."*[3]

This report on lacemaking in Ipswich was accompanied by details on the number of yards of lace of various values made in *"the Town of Ipswich, from August 1789 to August 1790: With the Value of the whole, computed from the Bartering-Prices at which the different parcels of each, have been sold."*[4] It shows that the 600 lace makers made 41,979 yards of lace worth 1869 pounds 8 shillings 10 pence at 1790 prices.[5] Mr. Dana suggests that after deducting about one third from the price of the lace (for mark-ups by the merchants) lace makers received about two thirds of the retail value, or approximately £1,270 collectively for one year's lace work.

---

[1] American Treasures of the Library of Congress, Democracy in America, Encouraging Manufactures for "Women & Girls". As accessed on 05.22.2017 on http://www.loc.gov/exhibits/treasures/tr11a.html#obj80 Scroll down to "Encouraging Manufactures for "Women & Girls". https://www.loc.gov/exhibits/treasures/trm157.html

[2] Letter from Joseph Dana to the Honorable George Cabot Esq of Beverly. July 26, 1790. *Industrial and Commercial Correspondence of Alexander Hamilton, Anticipating His Report on Manufactures*, edited by Arthur Harrison Cole, p 55. As accessed on 5.22.2017 on **https://babel.hathitrust.org/cgi/pt?id=wu.89094362027;view=1up;seq=93**

[3] Ibid p 56

[4] Ibid p 58

[5] Approximately $285,000 in 2017 US dollars as converted using http://www.uwyo.edu/numimage/currency.htm accessed on 05.22.2017

Included with the report to Alexander Hamilton were 36 actual samples of the lace. On Jan 24, 1791, the Reverend Dana wrote to Senator Cabot: *"You will receive, Sir, with this, some specimens of the work; And if returns are made to the Secretary by way of the Academy[6] it is asked as an indulgence, that these specimens, after being inspected by that honorable Body, may pass on, under their direction, so as to be ultimately presented to our beloved President of the United States, and to his Consort."* Of these lace samples, 22 were made with black silk, and 14 with white linen thread. The samples were never passed on to President Washington, but were kept with Alexander Hamilton's correspondence. Twenty-one of the black Ipswich lace samples made between August 1789 and August 1790 are preserved with Alexander Hamilton's papers at the Library of Congress, where they are available for study.

White linen laces were made in similar patterns in the late 1700s in Europe, but we do not know with certainty which patterns the Ipswich lace makers used with their linen thread, as the 14 linen samples made in 1789-90 and sent to Mr. Hamilton have not been located. The report from Mr. Dana on the laces made in Ipswich in the one-year period between August 1789 and August 1790 shows that two types of laces, referred to as "edgings" and "lace," were made. The edgings were cheaper, so most likely simpler than the wider, black laces, and probably made with linen thread. Black was fashionable in the late 18th century, and was also used for mourning attire. So, it is not surprising that there was demand for black lace to embellish shawls, hoods, and capes. The borders and edgings, such as the samples among Alexander Hamilton's papers, would have been used on these and other articles of clothing.[7]

Why Ipswich? The simple answer is that we don't know. It is well documented that textiles played an extremely important role in the early development and economy of North America. One thread of that storyline began in 1630, when the Massachusetts Bay Colony was settled by a group of about 700 English Puritans under the leadership of John Winthrop. Winthrop's son moved to a new area about 30 miles north of Boston in 1634, and renamed the existing Indian settlement Ipswich in honor of his home town in Suffolk, England.

In the early 1600s, lace was a common decoration among the citizens of the Massachusetts Bay Colony and a source of annoyance among some members of the ruling class. These attitudes can be learned from the Laws of the Massachusetts Bay Colony. Certain laws, called sumptuary laws, were passed between 1634 and 1651 to restrict which types of apparel were legal for each social class.[8]

From 1634: *"The Court, taking into consideration the great, superfluous, & unnecessary expenses occasioned by reason of some new & immodest fashions, as also the wearing of silver, gold, & silk laces… hath therefore ordered that no person, either man or woman, shall hereafter*

---

[6] American Academy of Arts and Sciences
[7] Museum of Fine Arts, Boston. collections/object/womans-hood-313741, and collections/object/womans-hooded-cloak-326482, as accessed on 05.22.2017 on http://www.mfa.org/collections/object/womans-hood-313741 and http://www.mfa.org/collections/object/womans-hooded-cloak-326482
[8] The Laws of the Massachusetts Bay Colony (1634-51) as accessed on 05.22.2017 on http://www.whrhs.org/cms/lib09/NJ01001319/Centricity/Domain/100/The%20Laws%20of%20Massachusetts%20Bay%20Colony.pdf

make or buy any apparel, either woolen, silk, or linen with any lace on it, silver, gold, silk, or thread, under the penalty of forfeiture of such clothes." In 1639, the law was repeated with the addition that *"no person whatsoever shall presume to buy or sell, within this jurisdiction, any manner of lace, to be worn or used within our limits."* It seems that the laws did not succeed in stopping *"excess in apparel, both of men and women…"* So, in 1651 a provision was added that *"No person…whose visible estates shall not exceed the true and indifferent value of 200 pounds shall wear any gold or silver lace, or gold buttons, or any bone lace above 2 shillings per yard…upon the penalty of 10 shillings for every such offense."* Bone lace is another name for bobbin lace.

So far, no specific evidence of lacemaking in Ipswich in the 1600s has come to light. It is clear from the laws that lace made with gold, silver, silk, and linen thread was being bought and sold, as well as worn. However, it may well all have been imported. Similar laces can be found in Europe from the same period.[9] We don't know who the initial lace teacher in Ipswich was, from where (s)he immigrated, or when (s)he arrived.

The lace pillows used in Ipswich were the large bolster style. The foot-side[10] of the lace was at the left (see note under technical details), and the bobbins were very simple, about four inches (10cm) long sticks whittled of bamboo, wood or local reeds. (See figures 1 and 2).

Fig. 1. *Ipswich lace pillow and bobbins. Catalog numbers E383685 and E383686 (Division of Home and Community Life, National Museum of American History, Smithsonian Institution)* Photo by Bev Wolov

This lace pillow (Fig. 1) was donated to the Smithsonian Museum by the great granddaughter of Elizabeth Lord Lakeman. Mrs. Lakeman was born in Ipswich, Massachusetts in 1767 and died in Hallowell, Maine, in 1862. She was a lace maker in the late 1700s and might have made the lace sample among Alexander Hamilton's papers that corresponds to the lace pattern that Mrs. Lakeman owned shown in fig. 4. She made lace on this pillow until her death and her last piece is still attached to the lace pillow (fig. 1). It is a fine Point Ground lace commonly made in the mid-19th century on both sides of the Atlantic.[11]

---

[9] Stevenow-Hidemark, Elisabeth (ed.), *1700-Tals Textil: Anders Berchs samling i Nordiska museet*, Nordiska Museet 1990, p. 221, and as accessed on 05.22.2017 on https://digitaltmuseum.se/search/?aq=descname%3A%22Spetsprovsamling%22
[10] Foot-side refers to the straight side of the lace that is meant for sewing onto fabric or clothing.
[11] Lace collection, Smithsonian. Scroll to *Ipswich Lace Pillow with Bobbins, Pattern, and Lace from Ipswich Massachusetts.* On 05.22.2017 accessed on http://americanhistory.si.edu/collections/object-groups/lace-collection?page=2

Mrs. Lakeman's lace pillow (fig. 1) went on display in the *Within These Walls...* exhibit when it opened in 2001 at the Smithsonian American History Museum. After being on display for a period, the lace pillow needed to be returned to rest in storage for preservation reasons, and I was asked to make a replica (fig. 3). It became a team effort with other volunteers. While I made the pattern and lace, Sheryl and John de Jong made the lace pillow, and Nick Carter whittled the bamboo bobbins. We purchased handmade brass pins. The pattern E386686 was chosen for the replica lace, as it is from Ipswich in the late 1700s, and corresponds to one of the lace samples in the Library of Congress (where I could study it).

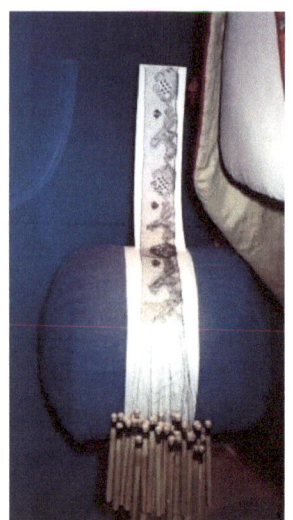

Fig. 2. *Replica lace pillow on display in the* Within These Walls... *exhibit at the Smithsonian American History Museum. Bobbin lace being made with black silk thread on a parchment copy of the Ipswich lace pattern from 1789-1790 is on the pillow. The lace pillow is stuffed with firmly packed straw and covered with two layers of linen fabric. Hand-whittled bamboo bobbins and handmade brass straight pins. (Division of Home and Community Life, National Museum of American History, Smithsonian Institution)*

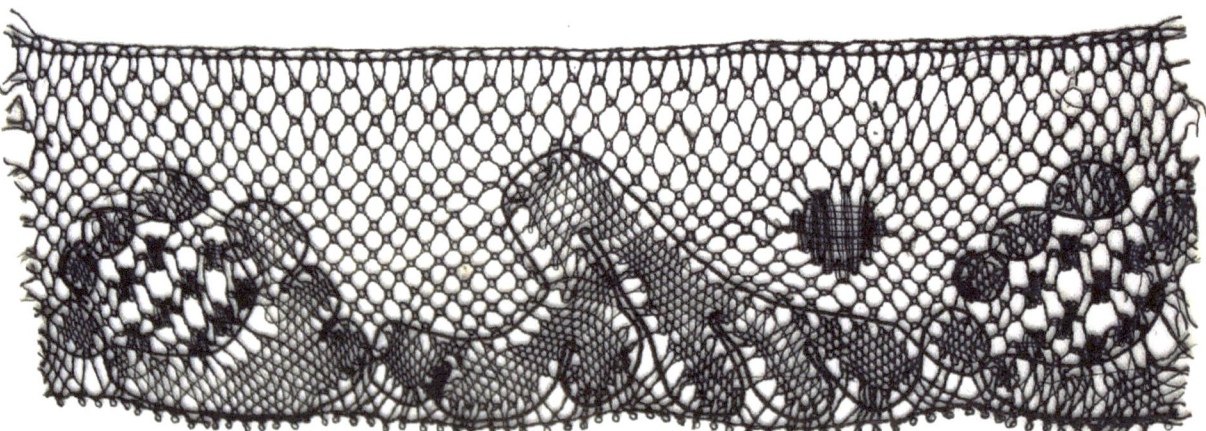

Fig. 3. *Bobbin lace sample made in Ipswich in 1789-1790, possibly by Elizabeth Lord Lakeman. Black silk. (Courtesy of the Library of Congress).*

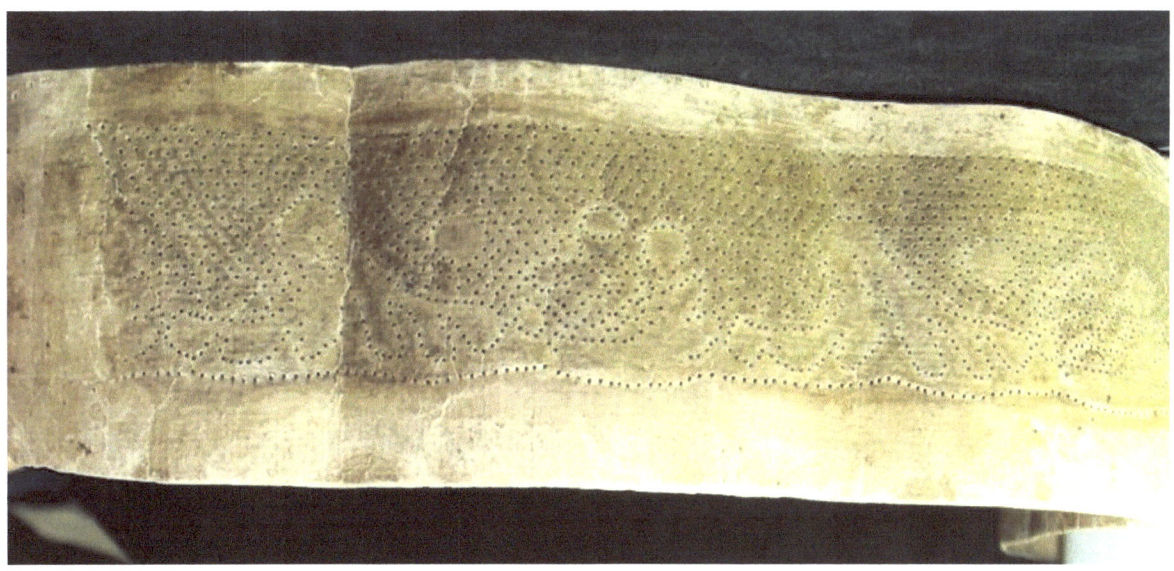

Fig. 4. *Pattern for bobbin lace made in Ipswich around 1790, corresponding to one of the lace samples among Alexander Hamilton's correspondence in the Library of Congress (#9), and used as a model for the replica lace in the* Within These Walls… *exhibit. Linen pasteboard. Catalog number E386686 (Division of Home and Community Life, National Museum of American History, Smithsonian Institution)* Photo by Bev Wolov

We know that lacemaking was well enough established in 1768 for some accounts to be settled by exchanging lace for other goods. In a merchant's account book from 1768, we find an entry for a Mr. David Pulsipher of Ipswich promising to pay for five yards of chintz with lace, which Mr. Pulsipher's family was granted five weeks to make and deliver.[12]

The listed prices for "edgings" are cheaper than the "laces." That indicates that edgings would have been simple, narrow laces, possibly made with linen thread; "laces" included the wider black silk laces, such as the samples among Alexander Hamilton's papers. The preserved black silk laces measure between 1 ¾ in. (4.4 cm) and 3 in. (7.3 cm) wide. The Ipswich Historical Society has a linen cap from 1795-98 with a simple linen lace edging, and the corresponding lace pattern for that edging.[13]

The surviving equipment from the Ipswich lace industry shows the laces were made on simple, round 30-inch circumference bolster pillows stuffed with seagrass. The fabric covers were made of coarse home-spun linen and covered with a second, replaceable layer of finer linen or cotton, or with pieced-together scraps from old clothing. The threads for the lace were wound on simple bobbins. Did someone in Ipswich specialize in making bobbin lace pillows and bobbins? We do not know, but the materials and characteristics of the surviving equipment suggest it was made locally, except for the pins and threads. The lace makers used a parchment

---

[12] Cotterell Raffel, Marta, *The Laces of Ipswich. The Art and Economics of an Early American Industry, 1750-1840* University Press of New England, 2003. p. 17

[13] Marta M. Cotterell, *Antiques Magazine*, December 1997, pp 858-859

or linen pasteboard[14] pattern that was long enough to encircle the bolster, and straight pins, which were handmade and very expensive at that point. The threads were either silk or linen. Both types of thread were probably imported from Europe, as the local silk thread production in the American colonies was not very successful. The American linen thread, while usable for weaving, was not even enough or fine enough for lace making.

The marketing and sales of the Ipswich laces were mostly done by relatives of the lace makers, as can be learned from various account books. The combination of bans on, or at least reluctance to buy, imported goods from England after the War of Independence and the popularity of decorating black shawls and other articles of clothing with lace made a perfect market for the Ipswich lace makers. They made enough lace to supply merchants in nearby towns and cities. Records show that the daughter of one of the lace makers made weekly trips to sell laces for Ipswich. From the sheer quantity of lace produced in 1789-1790, it can be assumed that many American women purchased and wore Ipswich lace. The 42,000 yards made during this one-year period alone would have been enough to ornament many capes, shawls and shirts. George Washington stopped in Ipswich in October 1789[15] and might have come away with lace for his wife, Martha, who cherished lace. A painting by Edward Savage of the Washington family in 1796 at the National Gallery of Art in Washington, DC[16], shows Martha Washington wearing a lacy shawl bordered with Ipswich style lace. A knitted black shawl, housed at Mt. Vernon, the estate of George and Martha Washington, is believed to have belonged to Martha Washington. It is also edged with black silk lace similar to the Ipswich samples.

The handmade bobbin lace industry continued in Ipswich into the early 1800s, but demand for lace diminished due to changes in fashion. Moreover, competition arose from the newly developed machine-made laces. Around 1809, a lace making machine, called the Old Loughborough or the Hand Circular, was invented by John Heathcoat in England. A few years later, parts of an Old Loughborough were smuggled from England to Ipswich and a machine was built there. The Boston and Ipswich Lace Company built a lace factory for making plain lace netting for embellishment (sometimes called bobbinet – not to be confused with fishing net) in Ipswich in 1824, and the New England Lace Company followed suit in 1828.[17] With the decline in demand for handmade bobbin lace, some of the local lace makers were employed to do embroidered (or "needle-run") decoration on the fine netting, and to get the finished lace ready to sell.[18] Both factories closed after a few years, but the handmade lace industry in Ipswich never recovered.

---

[14] Linen pasteboard is heavy paper "cardboard" made from 100% linen fibers.
[15] Joseph B. Felt, *History of Ipswich, Essex, and Hamilton*, 1834, reprint Ipswich, MA: Clamshell Press, 1966, p 206
[16] National Gallery of Art. Savage, Edward, The Washington Family (1789-1796). Accessed on 05.22.2017 on http://www.nga.gov/content/ngaweb/Collection/art-object-page.561.html
[17] Earnshaw, Pat, *Lace Machines and Machine Laces*, Batsford, 1986, 72-73
[18] Jesse Fewkes, *Fine Thread, Lace and Hosiery in Ipswich*, T. Frank Waters, *Ipswich Mills and Factories* Publications of the Ipswich Historical Society XIII, p. 19. Accessed on 05.22.2017 on
https://www2.cs.arizona.edu/patterns/weaving/books/archive_015.pdf

The goal of this book is to share the original lace samples made in Ipswich, Massachusetts during the year 1789 to 1790 with textile historians and lace makers who are interested in historical laces. In making the reproductions, I have strived to keep the motifs as close to the original sample as feasible, while making the "ground" more even than it is in the original samples. The "ground" refers to the plain net areas connecting the motifs, and was likely even in the original designs. I have constructed color-coded working diagrams as an aid to the lace maker. In addition, I hope the book suggests avenues for further exploration and research to expand our understanding of those important objects, as they represent both a "folly of fashion" and a uniquely documented trove of women's paid out-work[19] in the 18th and early 19th centuries.

For more information about the Ipswich Lace Industry see *The Laces of Ipswich. The Art and Economics of an Early American Industry, 1750-1840* by Marta Cotterell Raffel, University Press of New England, 2003.

---

[19] Women's paid out-work refers to paid work done by women in their homes for a factory.

All the original samples are made with black silk and are from 1¾" to 3" (4.4 cm to 7.3 cm) wide. Sample 5 is missing and samples 6 & 13 are incomplete pattern repeats. The photos show the entire length of each sample, but are not to scale. The numbers refer to numbers given by the Library of Congress. *Courtesy of the Library of Congress.*

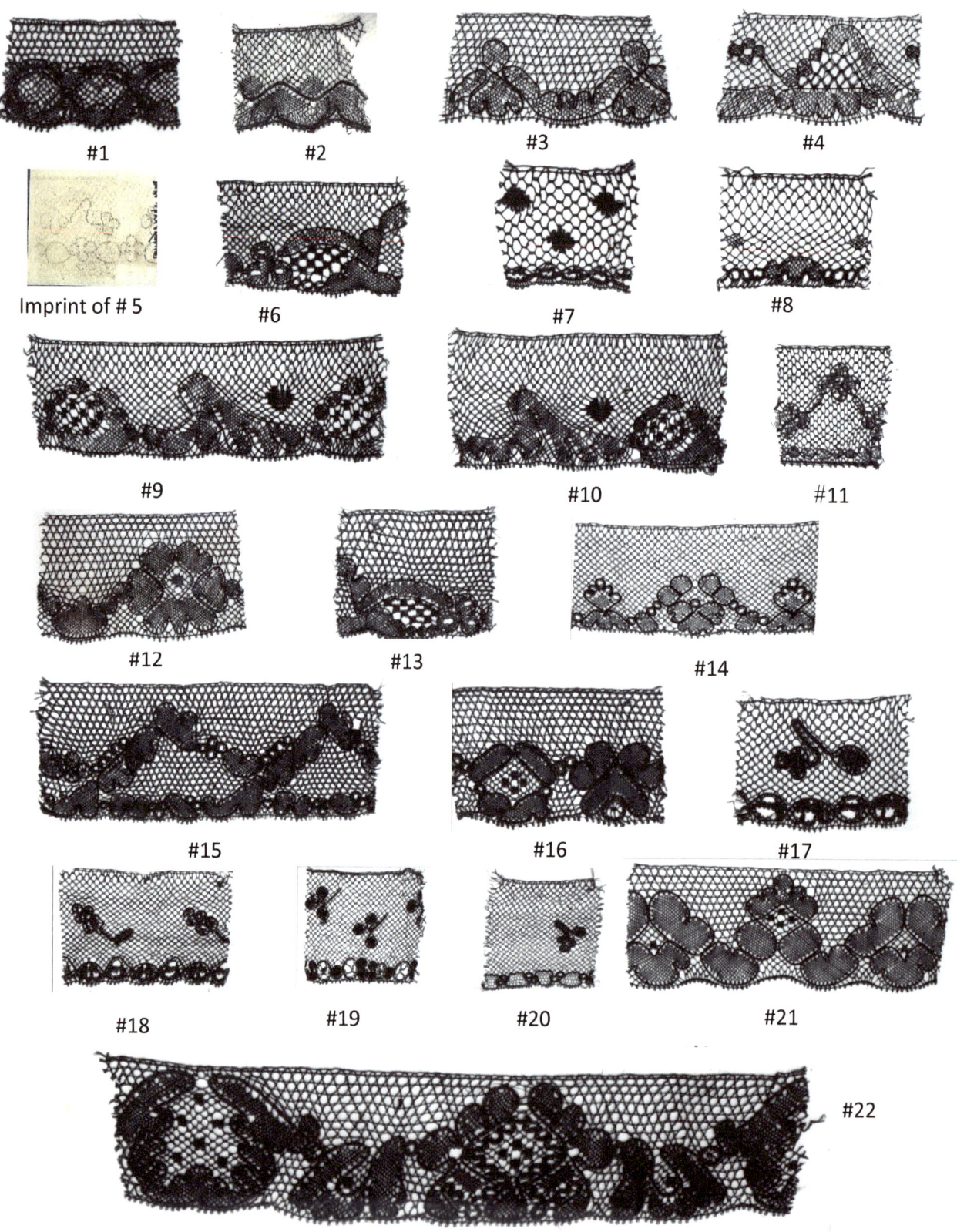

RECONSTRUCTED SAMPLES of IPSWICH LACE MADE 1789-1790 IN IPSWICH, MA
by Karen H. Thompson
The numbers are those assigned by the Library of Congress. Here arranged per style.

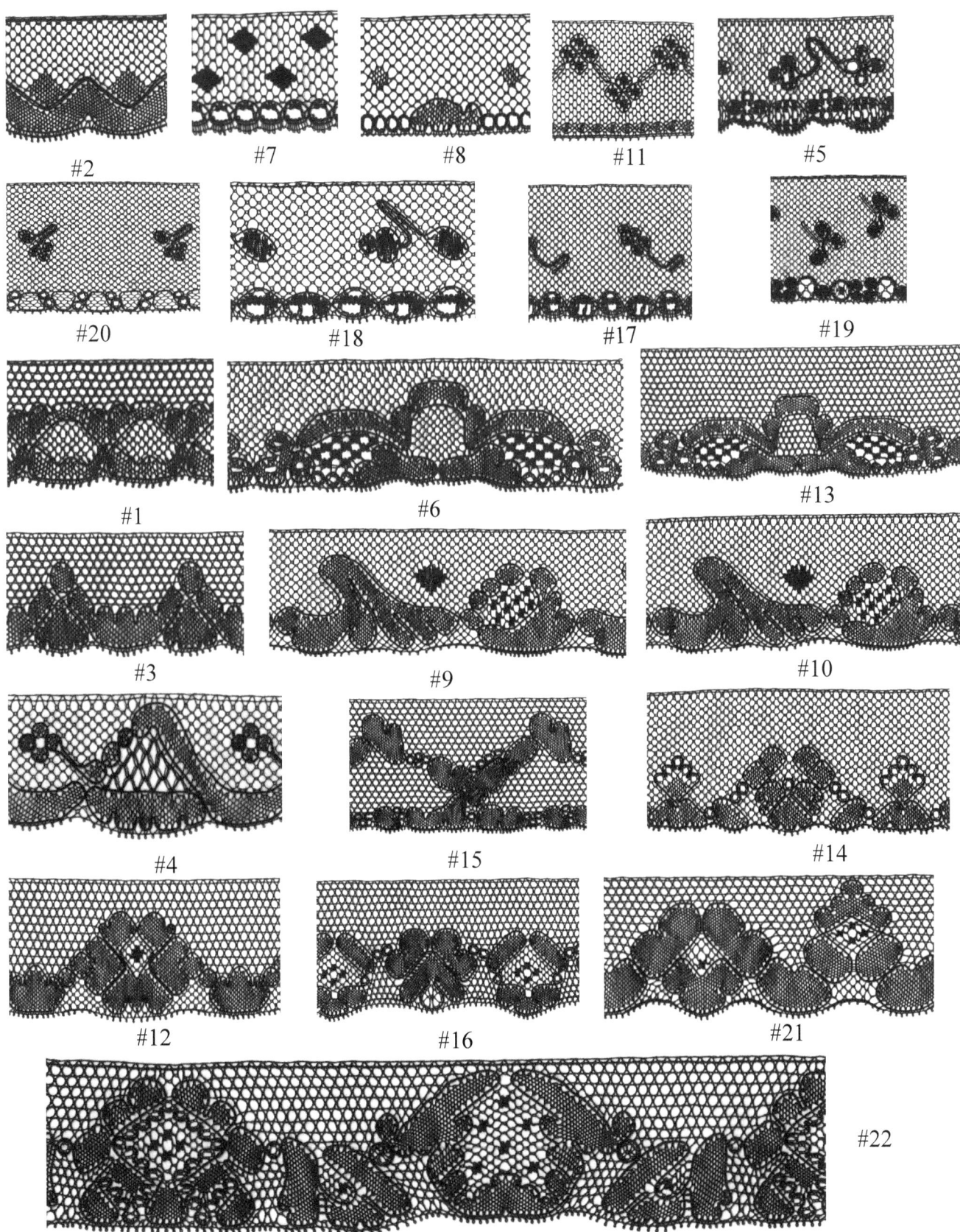

Technical Information about the Lace Samples and Making the Lace

Bobbin lace is a type of off-loom weaving, where the threads on four bobbins at a time are woven together to make the lace. Each bobbin lace stitch is made with two pairs of bobbins. Cross (c) means crossing the middle two bobbins from left to right from one pair to the other. Twist (t) means going right to left within each pair.

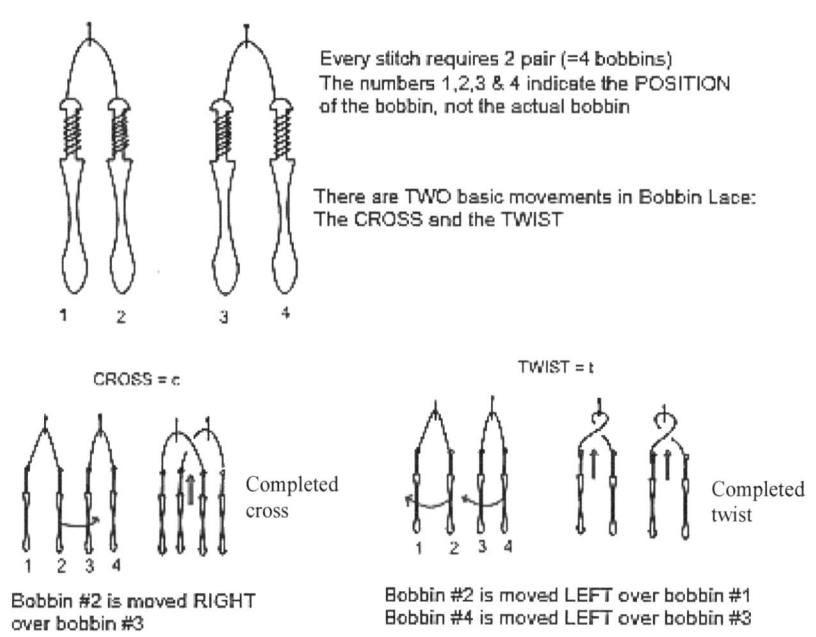

The Ipswich lace makers made lace on large, round bolster pillows. See fig. 1 and fig. 2. Most likely they used the "open" twist-cross sequence for the stitches, allowing the threads to hang parallel instead of twisted after each stitch. When making the working diagrams for the samples, I have used the "closed" cross-twist sequence, which is more common among lace makers in the US and elsewhere today, when using a flat, domed or roller pillow. The "open" and "closed" methods of making lace produce the same end results. Color coded working diagrams were developed around 1930, so would not have been available to the Ipswich lace makers in the late 1700s. They are added here as an aid to those lace makers who like to refer to them. Lace makers are encouraged to study the images of the samples and the corresponding pattern before starting a new pattern.

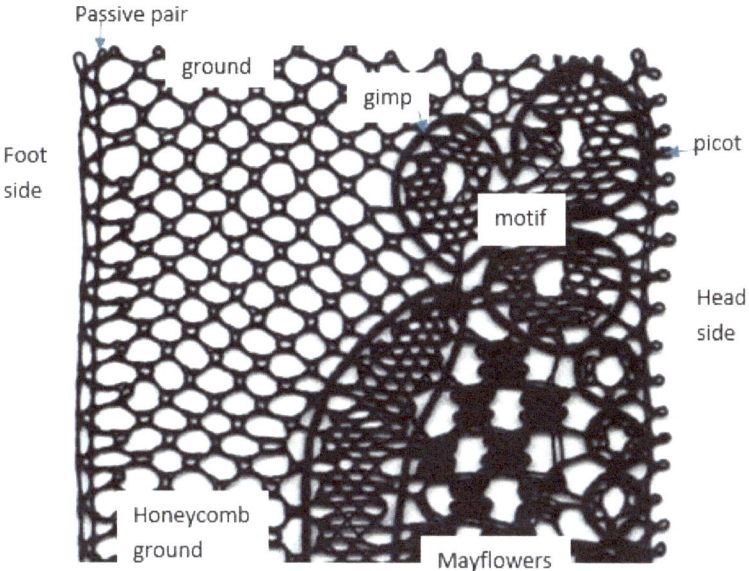

There are several common elements in the original samples:

The Ipswich laces are 'continuous' laces, using continuous threads from beginning to end. Some of the decorative elements, called motifs, are exceptions in which new outline or gimp threads are added at the beginning of the motifs and cut off at the end of the same motif.

Studying the direction of the gimp or outline thread in the separate motifs on the original samples shows that the straight sewing edge (foot side), was made on the left side of the lace.

Gimp thread(s) outline the motifs. Tracing the gimp paths before starting a new pattern is encouraged.

The samples all have one or more passive pairs at the foot side. The sewing edge, or foot side, is the side designed to be sewn onto fabric.

All samples have either two-thread twisted picots or "winkiepin" edges (two or more twists) at the decorated edge (head side). Most of the picots have approximately 5 twists around the pin, followed by 2 additional twists.

New threads were added by knotting in the original samples.

Small cloth-stitch squares, known as mayflowers, decorate some motifs.

The grounds are variations of the Torchon ground and include Honeycomb ground and the Kat-stitch, also called Paris ground. I chose to "true up" the grounds to make them more even, while maintaining the shape of the motifs as close as feasible to the original samples. All the samples are inconsistent in the number of twists in ground, edges and fillings. For the reconstructions, I have chosen to use the most common number of twists in most of the original samples. The exceptions are samples 1 and 22, which both have extra twists in the Kat-stitch ground.

All 21 Ipswich bobbin laces from 1789-90 among the Alexander Hamilton Manuscripts are edgings made with black silk. Most use a lightly-plied, three-ply, softly Z-spun thread for the thin lace thread, and one or two barely-plied, two-ply S-spun, thicker threads for the gimp. Both the fine thread and the gimp (outline) thread vary in size among the samples. Most of the samples have a gimp thread that is approximately four times as thick as the lace thread. Some samples use a thick gimp thread combined with a fine lace thread for the outlines. Where a gimp thread is used as the weaver or worker in some of the motifs, a thinner gimp thread is used, approximately three times as thick as the lace thread. In # 22, one black and one brown thread are combined for the gimp[20].

The angle in the ground varies a great deal within the same piece on most of the lace samples. This could be due to several factors. Among them are: distortion of the sample, distortion of the pattern (also called a pricking) from the original source from overuse or copying, or pins not being used in the ground. The pattern in fig. 4, for Ipswich sample #9, as well as a pattern at the Ipswich Museum for Ipswich #4 shows that pins were used in the honeycomb ground.

One of the original laces (#5) is missing. Reproduction of Ipswich #5 was made by studying the imprint on the original paper on which the now missing sample at the Library of Congress was mounted and a sample made by the late Michael Auclair in 1976 and preserved at the Ipswich Museum, Ipswich, MA. Mr. Auclair made exact reproductions of all 22 black silk samples, including the knots when adding a new thread, using black spun silk, which he reported was stiff compared to the very soft silk of the original samples. He used "twenty-year-old blue-print copies of the laces as copies"[21] to make his patterns, per an article written by Mr. Auclair in 1980.

---

[20] It is possible that the brown thread was black in 1789 and has faded to brown
[21] Letter written by Michael Auclair in New York City, February 1980. Author has photo copy of this letter from unknown source.

Two of the samples (# 6 and # 13) have only partially finished repeats. These two edgings have the same motifs but are of different widths and use different grounds. In each of these, I chose to add a mirror image of the available sample to make a full repeat. While I am quite sure that this is not the look of the original lace from which these patterns were made, I feel that is the best way to honor the original lace.

A few samples, such as # 15, have beginnings of pattern repeats. These show that the repeats are not identical, indicating that the lace maker sometimes solved the details of the design in different ways, and probably did not make the same lace over and over for years on end, but had to learn new patterns on a regular basis to keep up with demand for new lace designs.

While we do not know how the Ipswich lace makers got their patterns, some of them might have been skilled in making patterns from imported lace. This is one of the many areas that needs more research.

It should be noted that <u>point ground</u> (cross-twist-twist-twist pin or twist-twist-twist-cross pin) was first used as a ground very late in the 18th C, and was therefore a relatively new technique when it was used as a filling in # 20.

The lace samples range in width from approximately 4.4 cm (1¾") to 7.3 cm (3") (See p. 21)

The original samples from 1789-1790 have been remounted on acid-free backing, covered with Mylar, numbered, and are available for study at the Library of Congress.

The black silk threads used for the reproduced samples are Clover 50, (3-ply, Z-spun, size approximately 36-38 wraps per cm) and Gütermann 30/3 (S1003, 3-ply, Z-spun, size approximately 16 wraps per cm) for gimp. Kreinik Soie Perlee or double thickness of the lace thread is used for a thinner gimp thread.

To calculate the number of wraps per centimeter, wrap the thread around a ruler or pencil and count how many threads lie snugly side by side in one centimeter. Among other possible thread choices are YLI 50, Piper's Silks spun silk 130/3, 140/2, Tire silk Machine twist 50, and The Winner machine silk.

_____

Working Diagrams

Note: Working diagrams are made for "closed" method: c-t-c-t.
The Ipswich lace makers probably used the "open" method: t-c-t-c.
Please adjust to your preferred method.

- c-t-c-t
- c-t-c
- c-t-c with gimp pair
- c-t
- gimp with 1-2 twists each side
- picot with double threads, mostly with 5 twists
- extra twist
- Support pin (optional)
- + Add gimp

Recommendation: Trace gimp paths before starting

#1: Ground in original sample: c-t-c-t-t-t

#22: Ground in original sample: c-t-c-t-t

#2, #22: Use thinner gimp pair or double lace thread for passive pair at foot side use thinner gimp such as Soie Perlee, or 3 times the thickness of the lace thread as the worker in motifs.

#7 and #19: #20: 2 twists in picot

#4 spider: first half as usual. Pin, c-t-c outside pairs on both sides, tw left pr, c-t-c center pr

Overview of dimensions and some common elements in the original samples

Sample number	Width	Length	Ground: Most consistently used. c = Cross, t = twist	Picots/edge
1	4.4cm (1.7")	7cm (2.8")	c-t-c-t-t-t Kat stitch (Paris Ground)	Picots 3 twists (t)
2	4.7cm (1.9")	6cm (2.4")	c-t-c-t-t pin c-t-t	Picots 3-5 t
3	4.8cm (1.9")	8.5cm (3.4")	c-t-c-t or c-t-c-t-t Kat stitch	Picots 3-5 t
4	5cm (2")	9cm (3.5")	c-t-t pin c-t-t	Picots 1-3 t
5	Missing ≈5cm (2")	≈ 8.7cm (3.5)"	c-t-t pin c-t-t	Picots 3-5 t
6	5.2cm (2")	8.3cm (3.3")	c-t-t pin c-t-t	Picots 1 t
7	5cm (2")	5.3cm (2.1")	c-t-c-t pin c-t-c-t-t	c-t-c-t pin c-t-c-t extra t on worker
8	5.3cm (2.1")	7cm (2.8")	c-t-c-t pin c-t-t, or c-t-c-t pin c-t-t-t, or c-t pin c-t-t	c-t-c-t-t pin c-t-c-t-t
9	5cm (2")	15cm (5.9")	c-t-t pin c-t-t	Picots 3-5 t
	6cm (2.4")	12cm (4.7")	c-t-t pin c-t-t	Picots 1-3 t
11	6.6cm (2.6")	5.8cm (2.3")	c-t-c-t pin c-t-c-t-t	Picots 3-5 t
12	6.6cm (2.6")	10.7cm (4.2")	c-t-c-t Kat stitch	Picots 5 t
13	6.7cm (2.6")	7.5cm (3")	c-t-c-t Kat stitch	Picots 5 t
14	6.3cm (2.5")	14 cm (5.5")	c-t-t pin c-t-t	Picots 5 t
15	6.7cm (2.6")	16 cm (6.3")	c-t-c-t Kat stitch	Picots 3-5 t
16	5.7cm (2.2")	8.6cm (3.4")	c-t-c-t Kat stitch	Picots 1 t
17	6.5cm (2.6")	9.1cm (3.6")	c-t-t pin c-t-t	Picots 1-3 t
18	5.8cm (2.3")	7.3cm (2.9")	c-t-t pin c-t-t	Picots 5 t
19	7.3cm (2.9")	7.5cm (3")	c-t-t pin c-t-t	Picots 1-3 t
20	6.5cm (2.6")	6.5cm (2.6")	c-t-t pin c-t-t	Picots 1-3 t
21	6.7cm (2.6")	17.3cm (6.8")	c-t-c-t or c-t-c-t-t Kat stitch	Picots 5 t
22	5.2cm (2")	22cm (8.7")	c-t-c-t or c-t-c-t-t Kat stitch Filling c-t-c-t-t pin c-t-t	Picots 5 t

Reconstructed Patterns and Working Diagrams for the

Ipswich Samples from 1789-1790

By

Karen H. Thompson

IPSWICH sample #2 made in Ipswich 1789-1790
Size of original sample:
4.7 cm (1.9") wide, 6 cm (2.4") long

Original sample

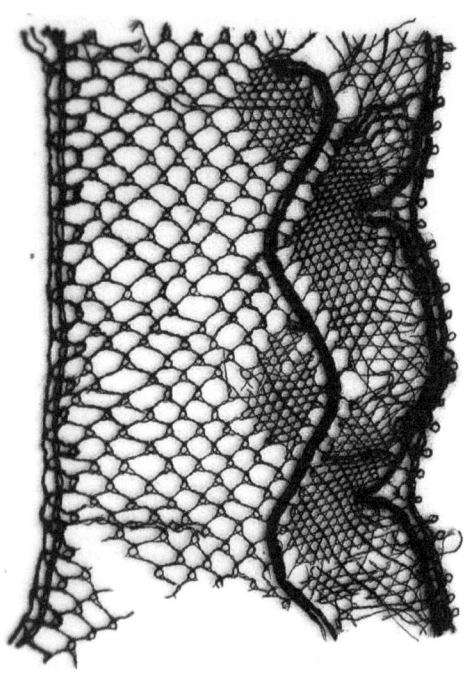

IPSWICH #2 reproduction
Width of lace is 4.7 cm (1.9")
one repeat is 3.3 cm (1 ¼") long

Reproduction

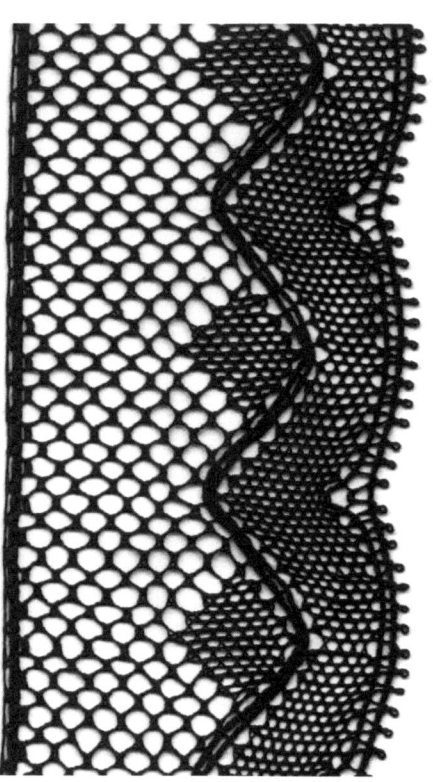

IPSWICH sample #2 made in Ipswich 1789-1790
Reconstructed sample by Karen H. Thompson, 2015
25 pairs + 1 thicker thread for foot side passive
+4 single gimp threads (or 2 pairs)
For correct size, one repeat of the pricking is
3.3 cm or 1 ¼" long

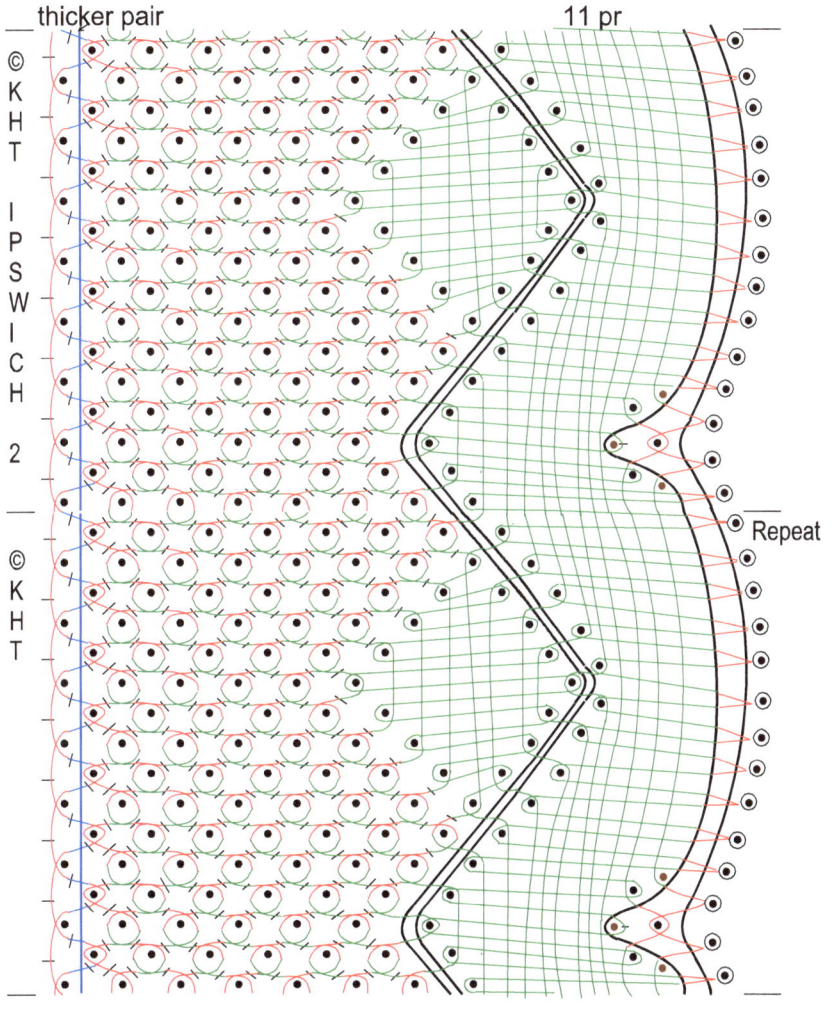
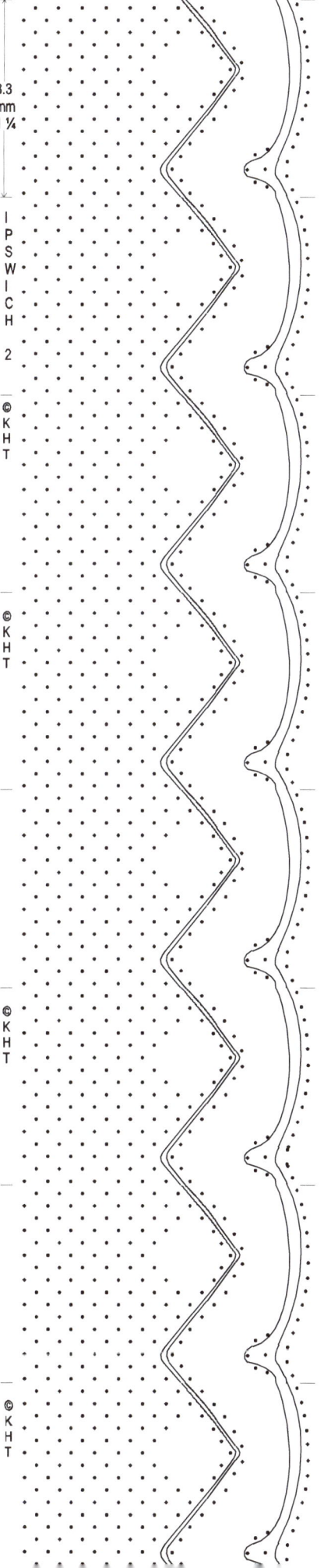

25

IPSWICH sample #7 made in Ipswich 1789-1790
Size of original sample:
5 cm (2") wide, 5.3 cm (2.1") long

Original sample

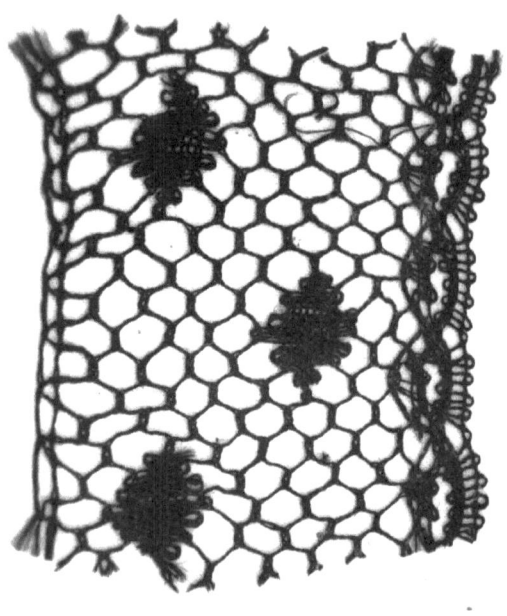

IPSWICH #7 reproduction
Width of lace is 5 cm (2")
one repeat is 3.1 cm (1 3/16") long

Reproduction

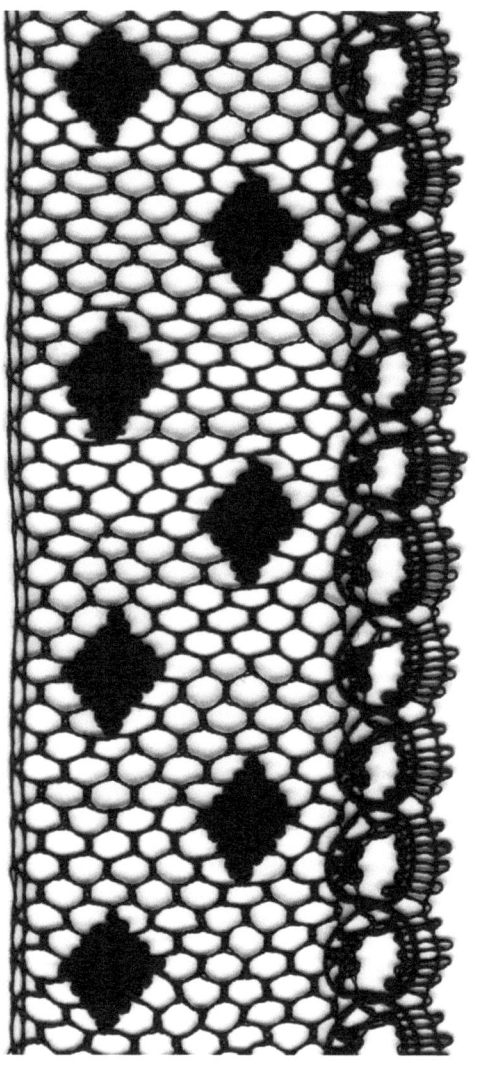

IPSWICH sample #7 made in Ipswich 1789-1790
Reconstructed sample by Karen H. Thompson, 2015
22 pairs + 1 pair gimp
+ 1 pair thinner gimp thread for the diamond motifs
For correct size, one repeat of the pricking is
3.1 cm or 1 3/16" long

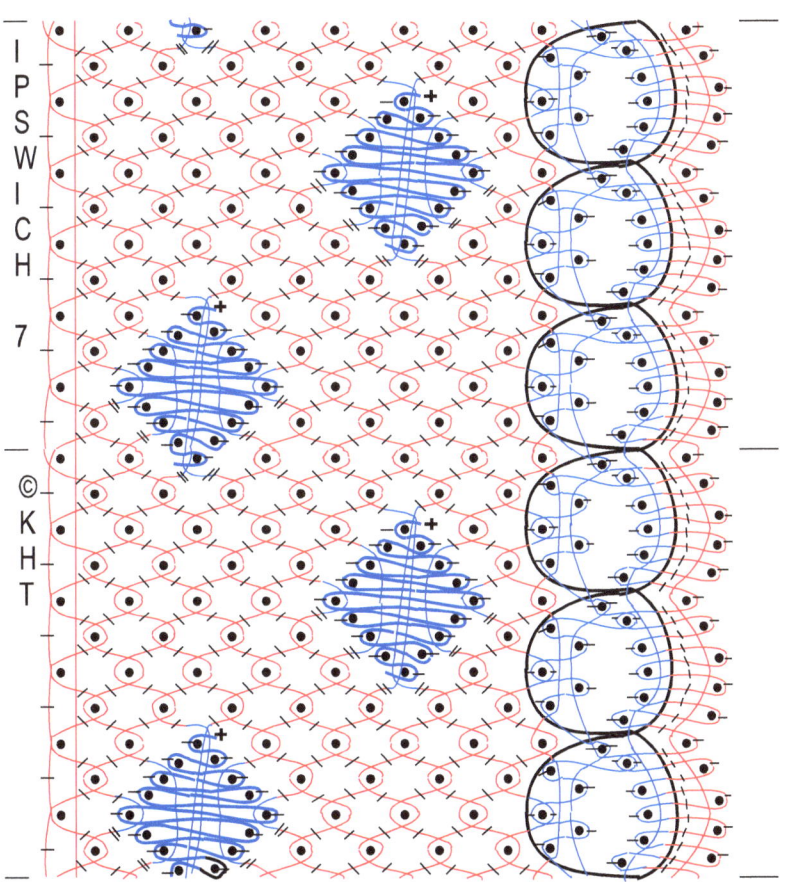
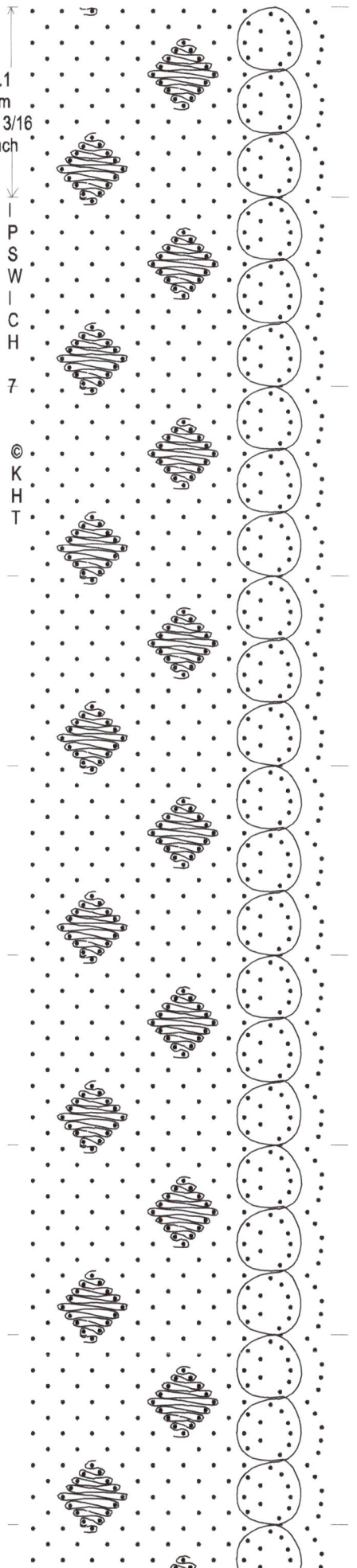

IPSWICH sample #8 made in Ipswich 1789-1790
Size of original sample:
5.3 cm (2.1") wide, 5.3 cm (2.1") long

IPSWICH #8 reproduction
Width of lace is 5.3 cm (2.1")
one repeat is 5.7 cm (2 ¼") long

Original sample

Reproduction

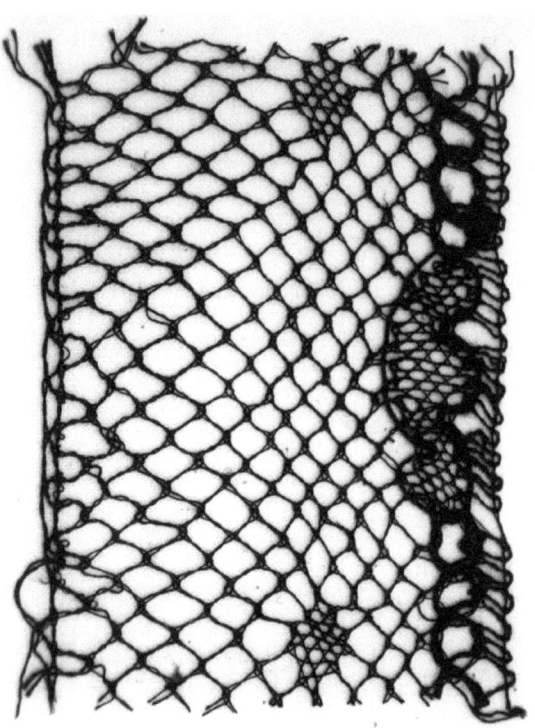
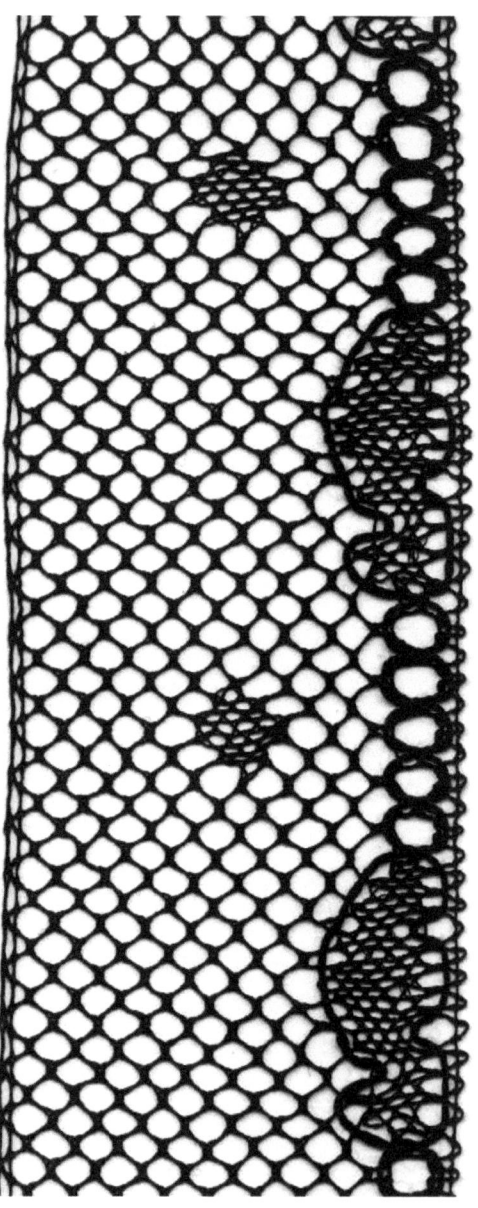

IPSWICH sample #8 made in Ipswich 1789-1790
Reconstructed sample by Karen H. Thompson, 2015
23 pairs + 1 pair gimp
For correct size, one repeat of the pricking is
5.7 cm or 2 ¼" long

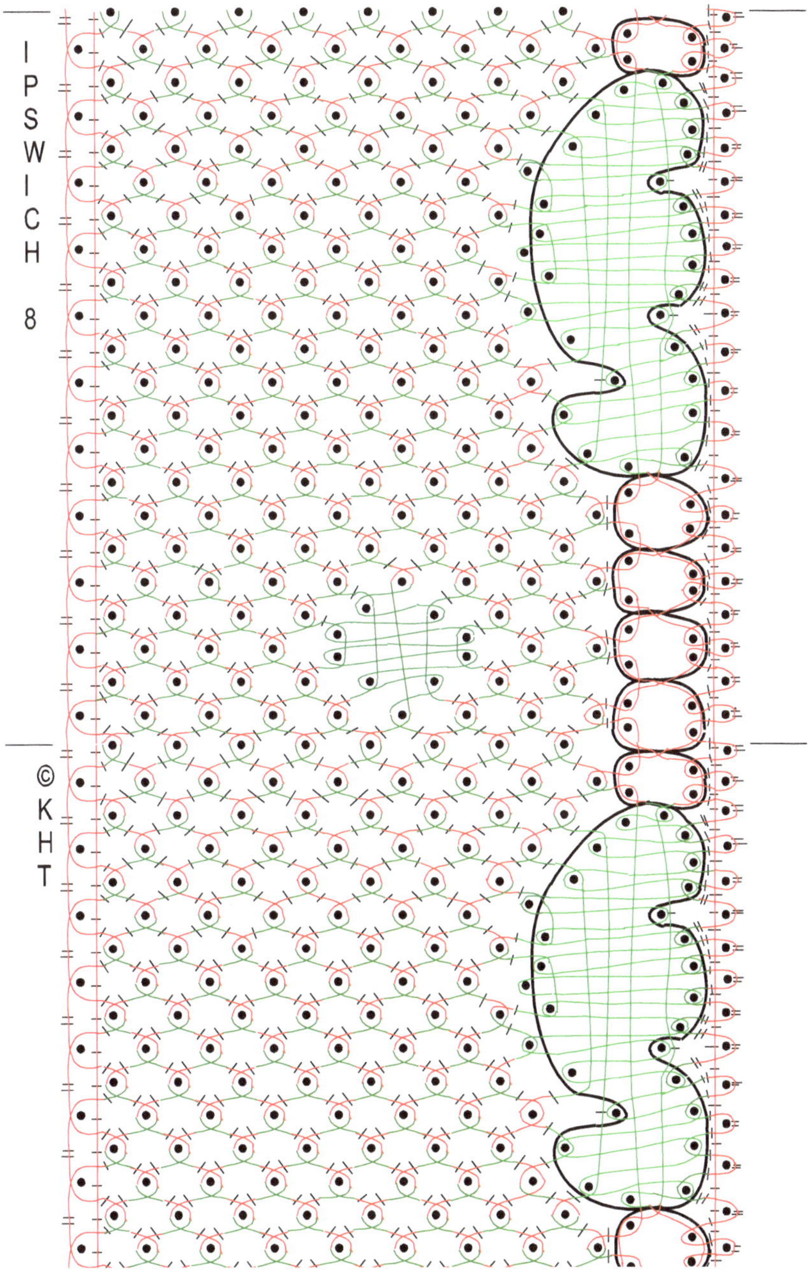

IPSWICH sample #11 made in Ipswich 1789-1790
Size of original sample:
6.6 cm (2.6") wide, 5.8cm (2.3") long

Original sample

IPSWICH #11 reproduction
Width of lace is 6.6 cm (2.6")
one repeat is 5.4 cm (2 1/16") long

Reproduction

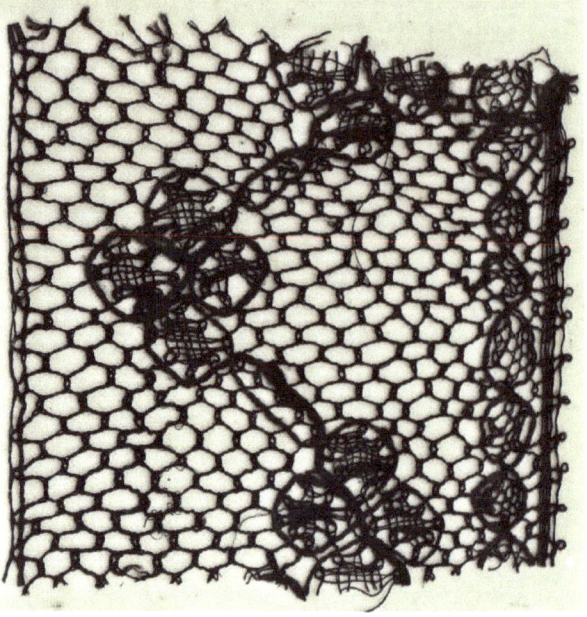
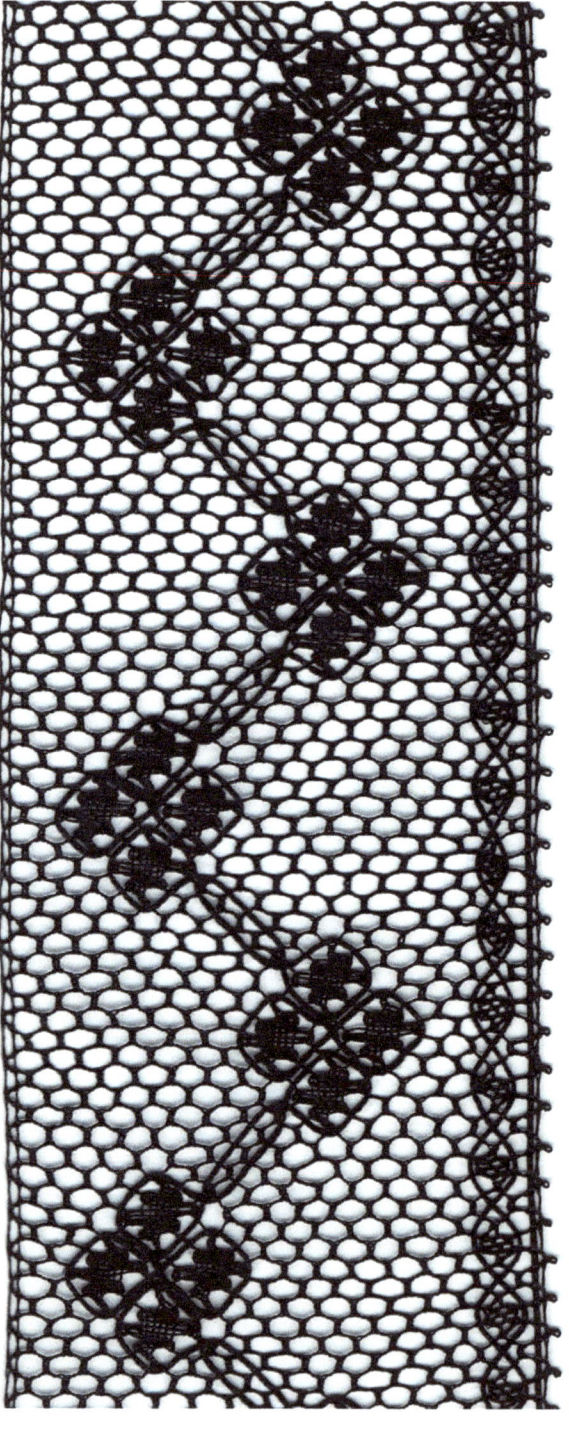

IPSWICH sample #11 made in Ipswich 1789-1790
Reconstructed sample by Karen H. Thompson, 2016
34 pairs + 2 pair gimp
For correct size, one repeat of the pricking is
5.4 cm or 2 1/16" long

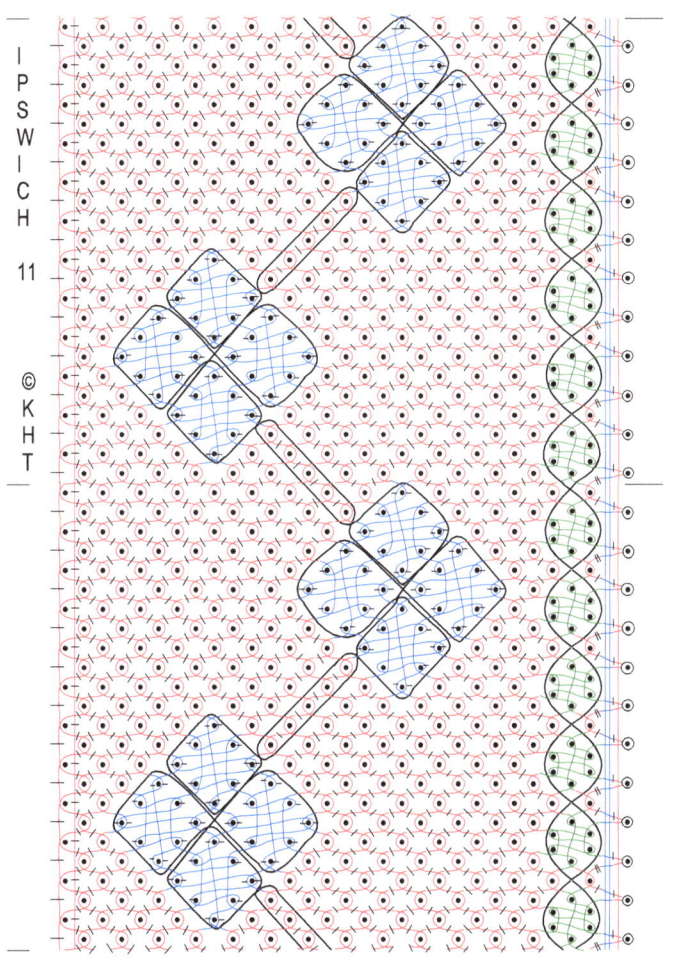

gimp paths

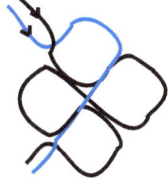

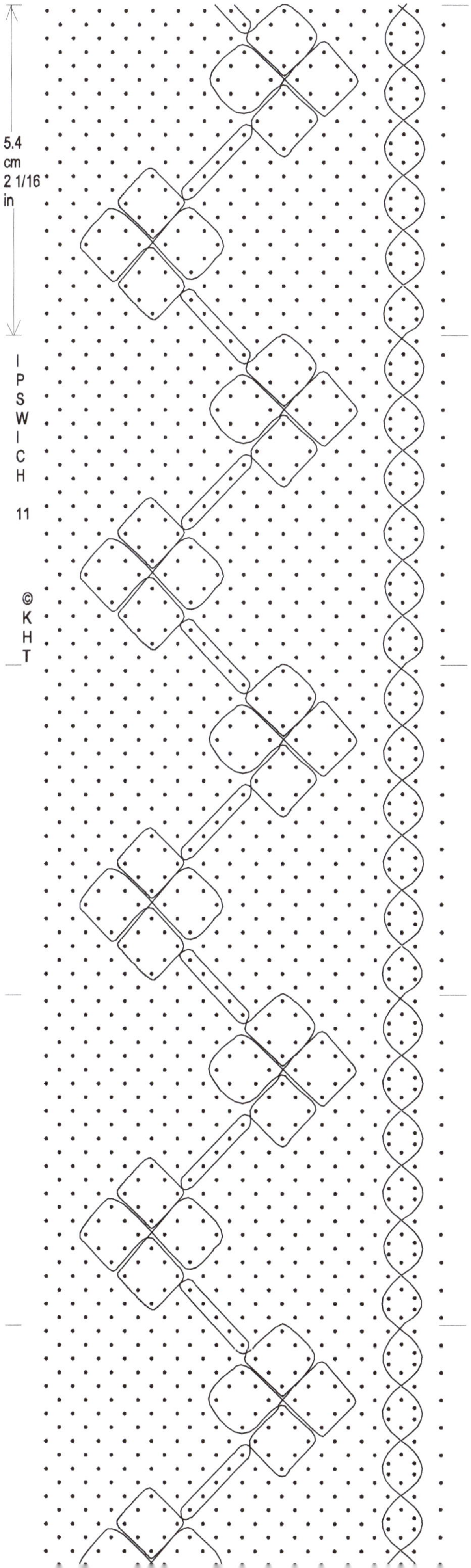

IPSWICH sample #5 made in Ipswich 1789-1790
Size of imprint on paper on which it was mounted:
~ 5.2 cm (2") wide, 8.7 cm (3.5") long

Imprint of original sample

Reproduction by Michael AuClair 1976

IPSWICH #5 reproduction
Width of lace is 5.2 cm (2")
one repeat is 6.6 cm (2 9/16") long

Reproduction by author

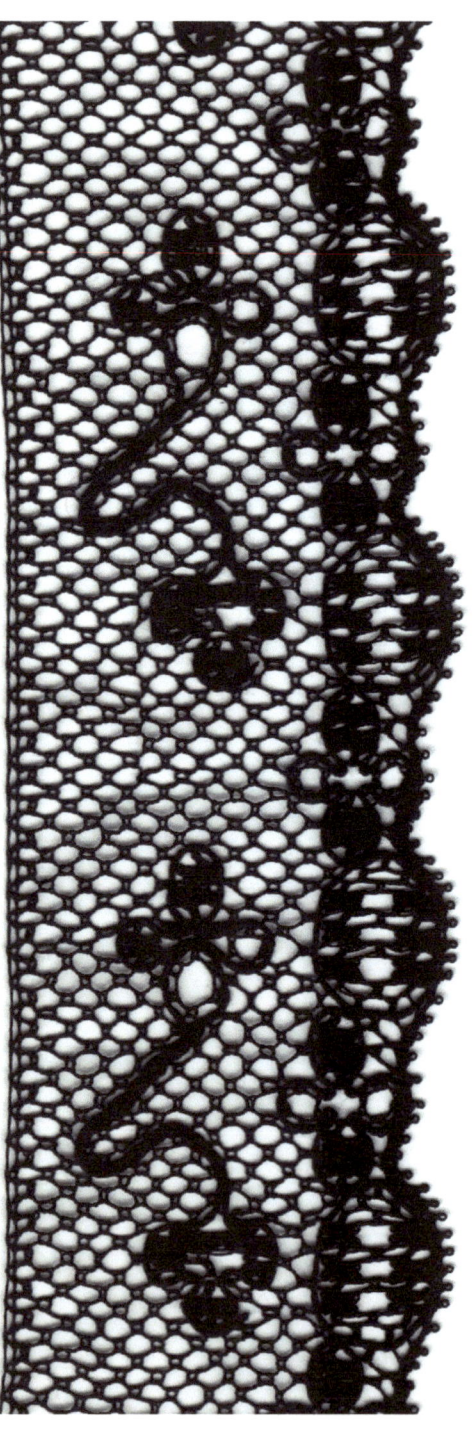

IPSWICH sample #5 made in Ipswich 1789-1790
Reconstructed sample by Karen H. Thompson, 2015
27 pairs + 2 pairs gimp threads
For correct size, one repeat of the pricking is
6.6 cm or 2 9/16" inches long

IPSWICH sample #20 made in Ipswich 1789-1790
Size of original sample:
6.5 cm (2.6") wide, 6.5 cm (2.6") long

IPSWICH #20 reproduction
Width of lace is 6.5 cm (2.6")
one repeat is 7 cm (long

Original sample

Reproduction

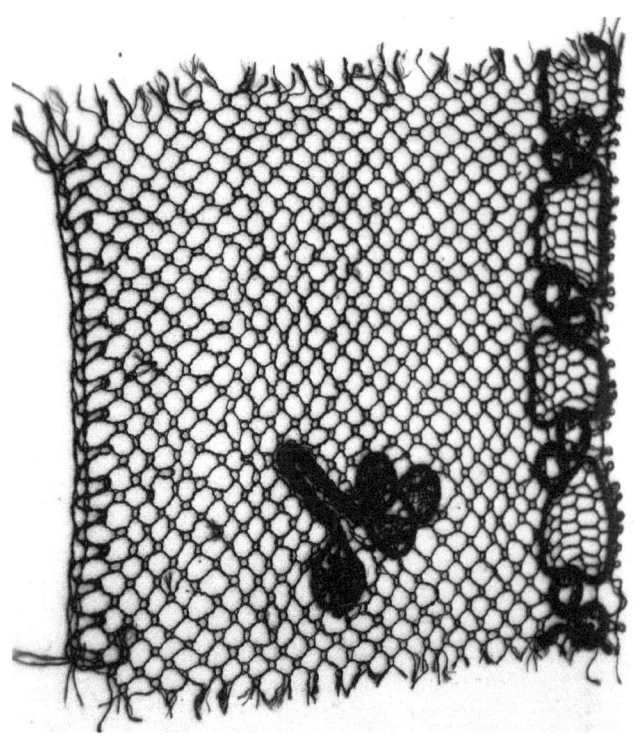
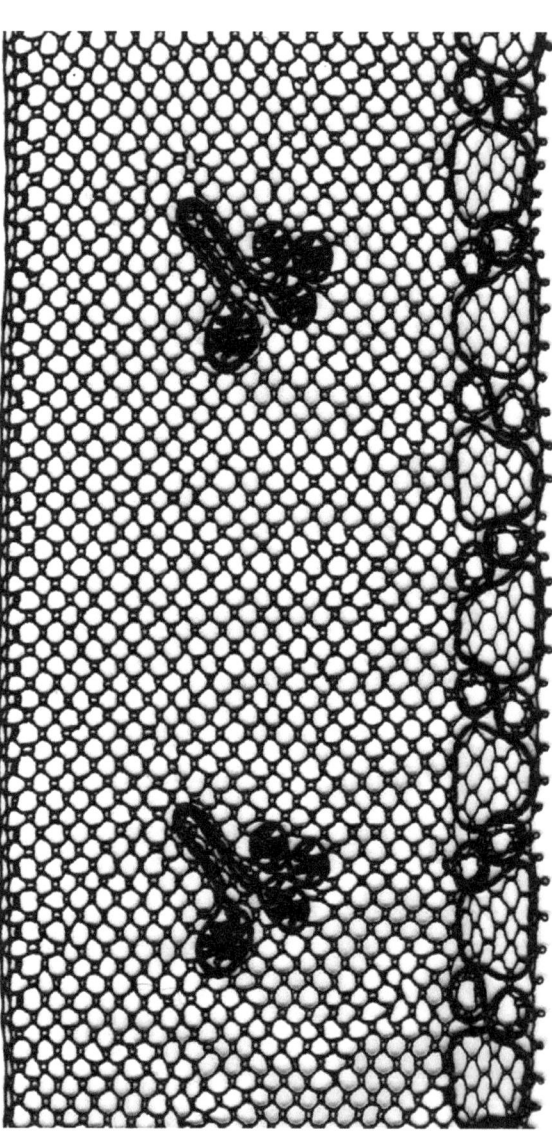

IPSWICH sample #20 made in Ipswich 1789-1790
Reconstructed sample by Karen H. Thompson, 2016
45 pairs + 2 pair gimp
For correct size, one repeat of the pricking is
7 cm or 2 ¾" long

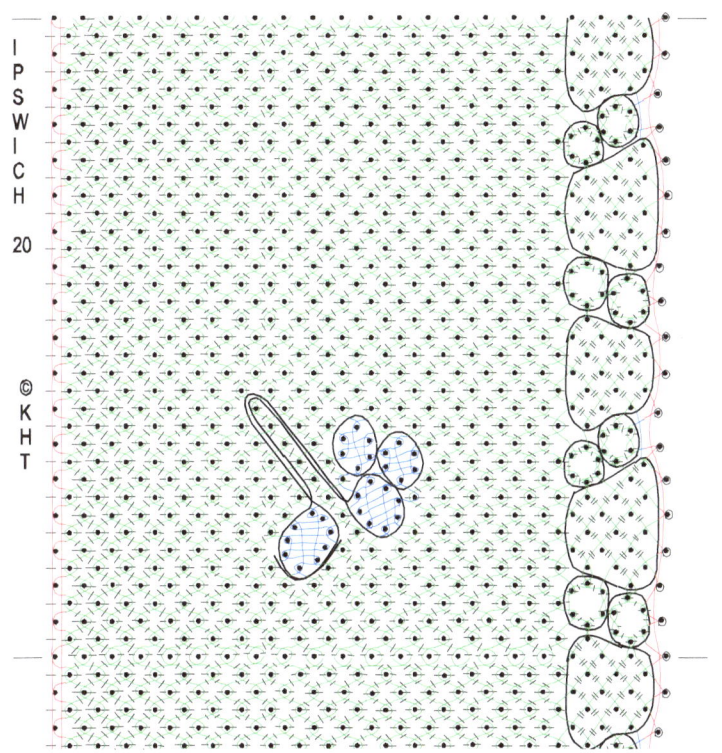

gimp paths

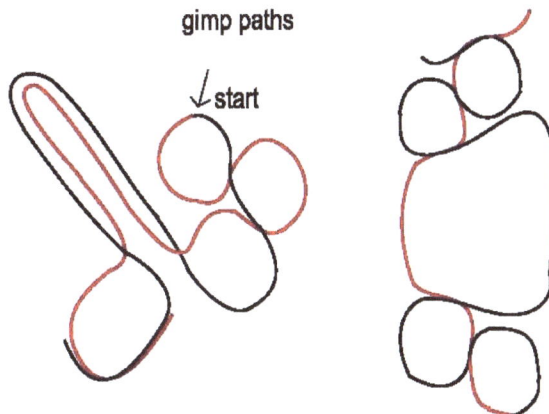

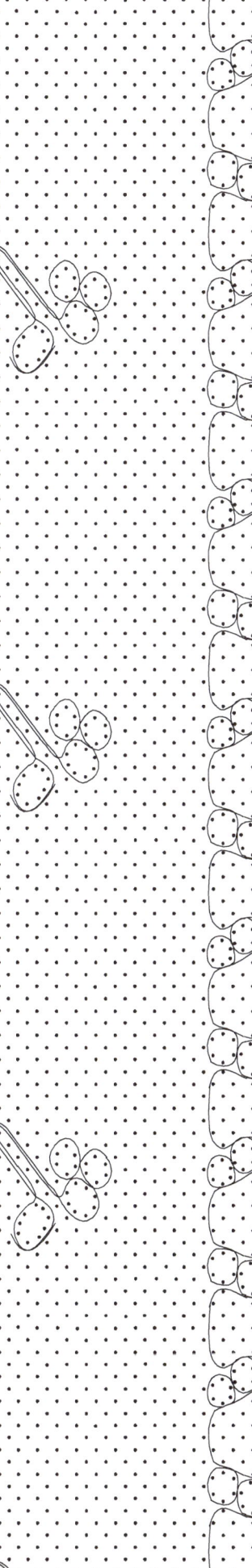

IPSWICH sample #18 made in Ipswich 1789-1790
Size of original sample:
5.8 cm (2.3") wide, 7.3 cm (2.9") long

IPSWICH #18 reproduction
Width of lace is 5.8 cm (2.3")
one repeat is 7.6 cm (3") long

Original sample

Reproduction

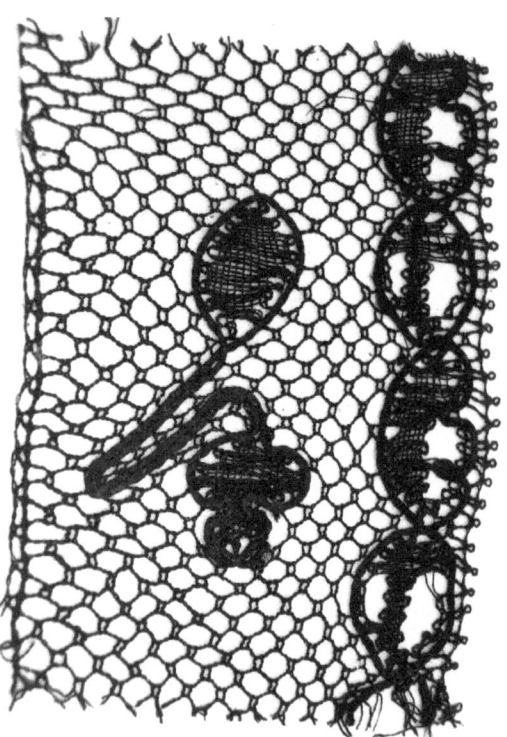

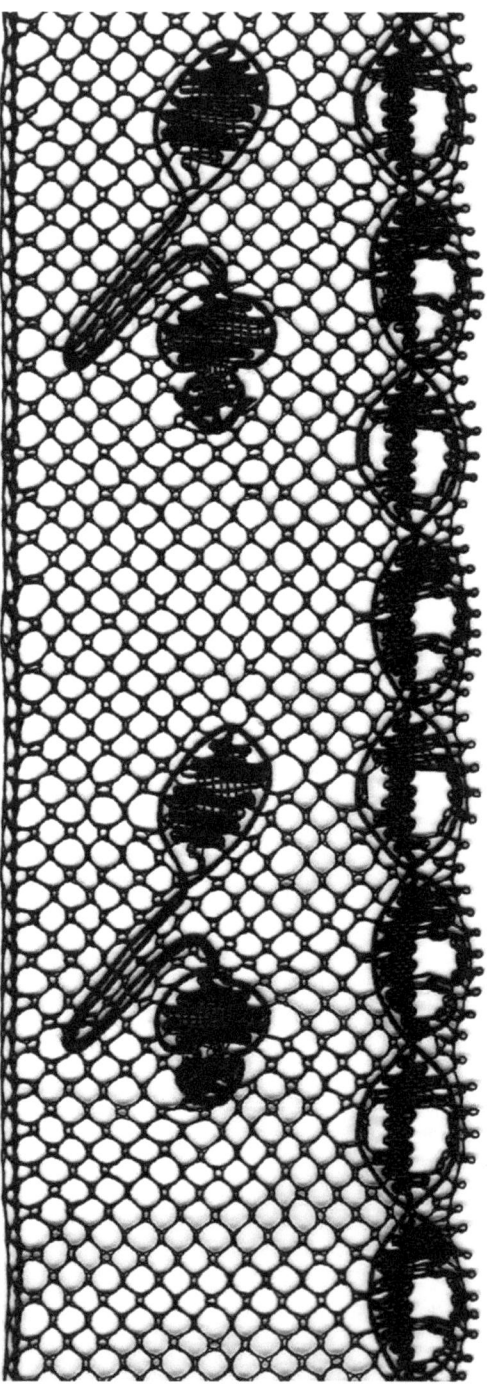

IPSWICH sample #18 made in Ipswich 1789-1790
Reconstructed sample by Karen H. Thompson, 2016
28 pairs + 2 pair gimp
+ 1 thin pair gimp for passive pair at foot side
For correct size, one repeat of the pricking is
7.6 cm or 3" long

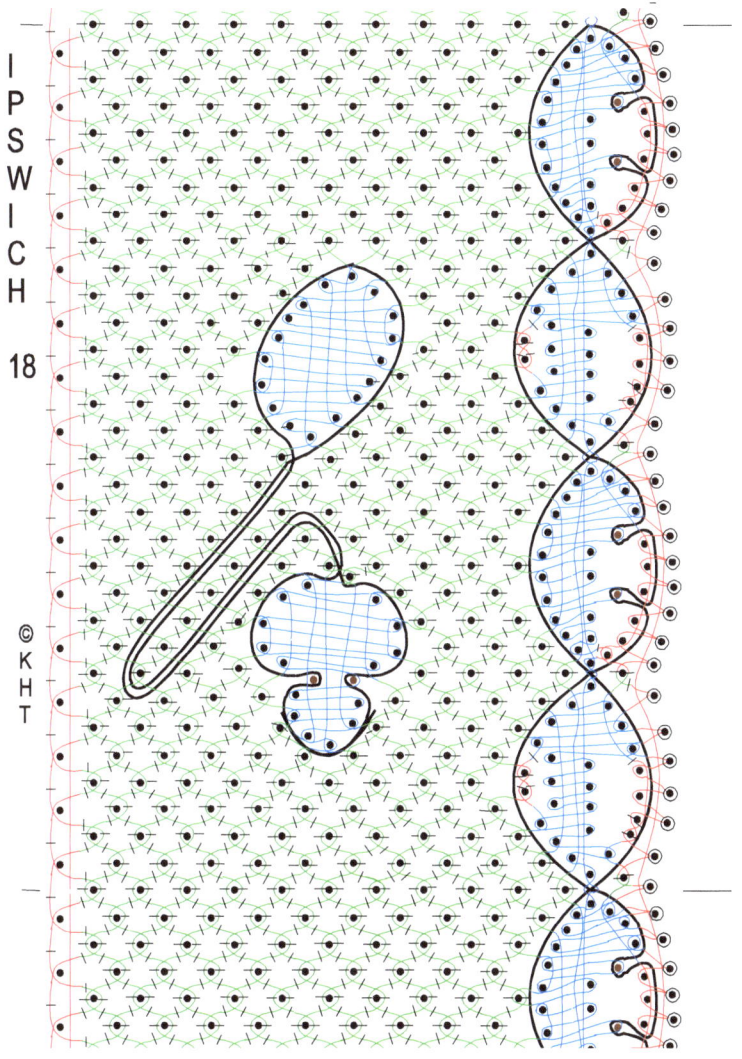
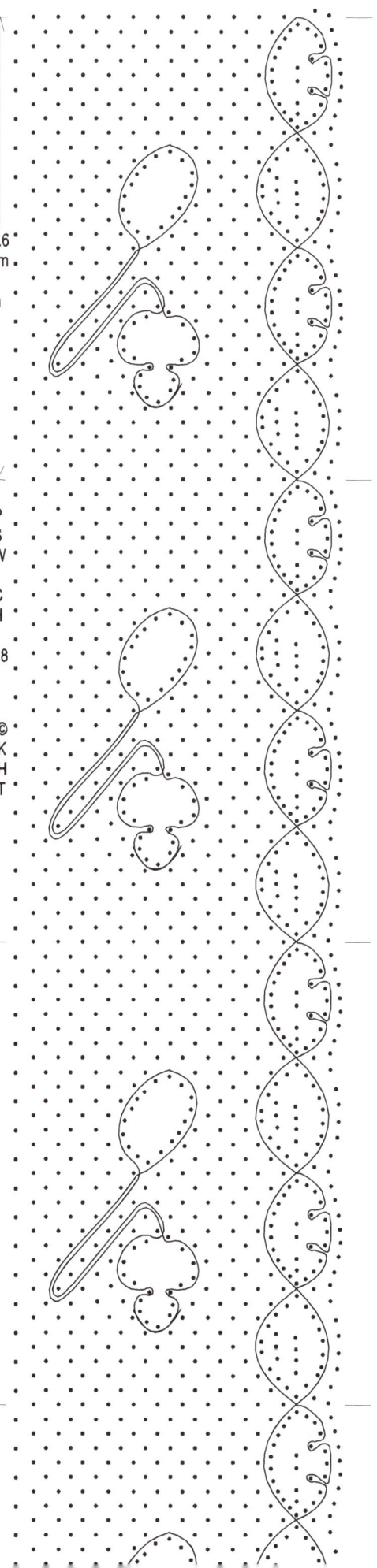

37

IPSWICH sample #17 made in Ipswich 1789-1790
Size of original sample:
6.5 cm (2.6") wide, 9.1 cm (3.6") long

IPSWICH #17 reproduction
Width of lace is 6.5 cm (2.6")
one repeat is 5.7 cm (2 ¼") long

Original sample

Reproduction

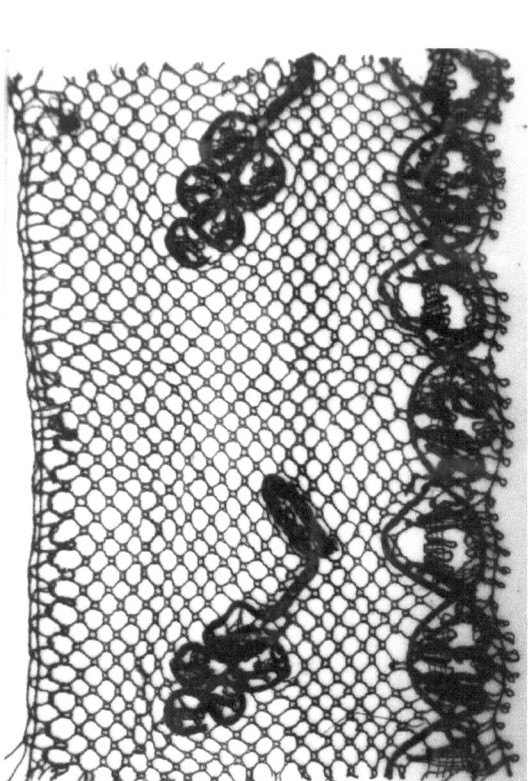
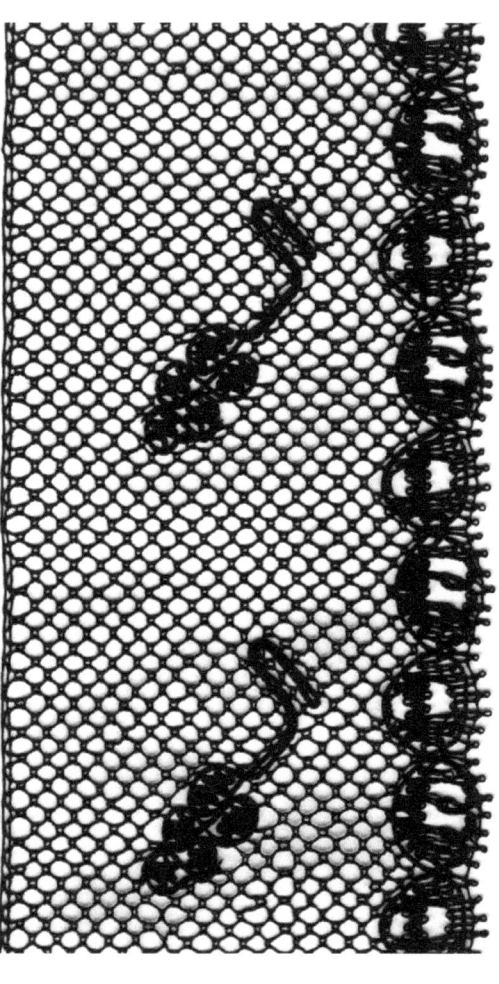

IPSWICH sample #17 made in Ipswich 1789-1790
Reconstructed sample by Karen H. Thompson, 2016
38 pairs + 2 pair gimp
For correct size, one repeat of the pricking is
5.7 cm or 2 ¼" long

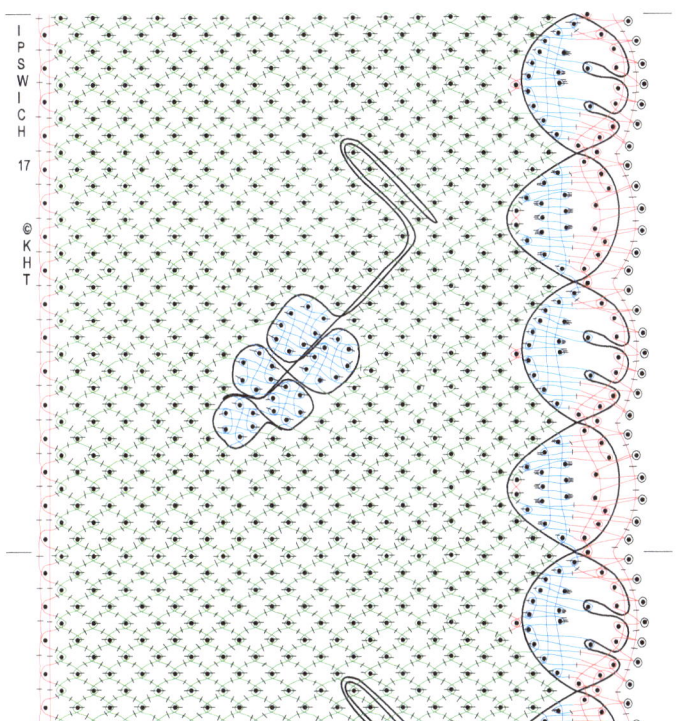

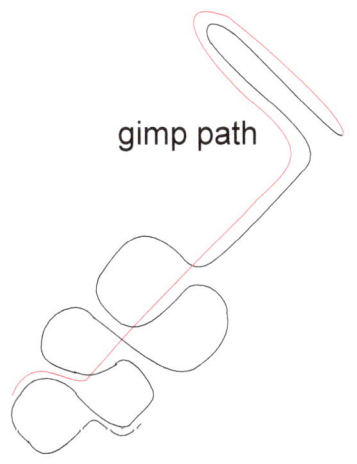

gimp path

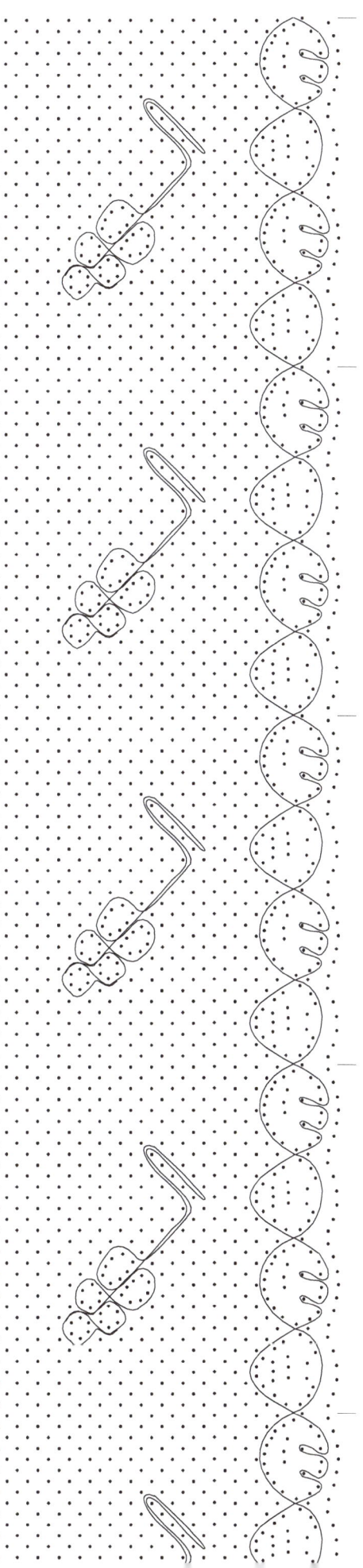

IPSWICH sample #19 made in Ipswich 1789-1790
Size of original sample:
7.3 cm (2.9") wide, 7.5 cm (3") long
long

Original sample

IPSWICH #19 reproduction
Width of lace is 5.8 cm (2.3")
One repeat is 14.3 cm (5 5/8")

Reproduction

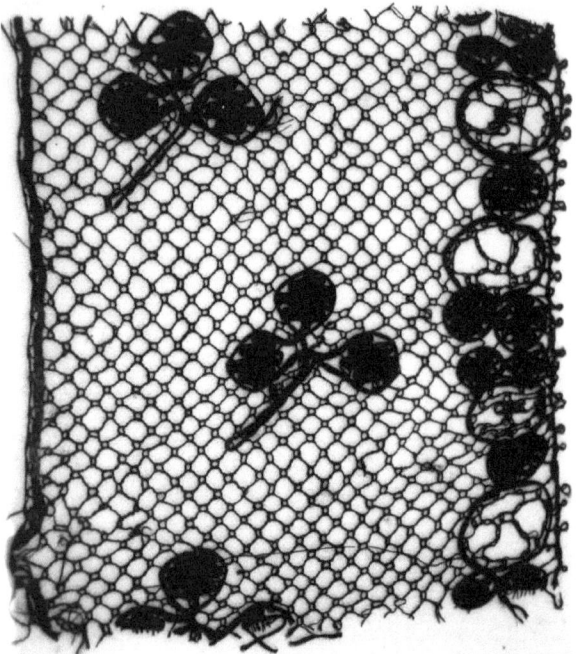

IPSWICH sample #19 made in Ipswich 1789-1790

Reconstructed sample by Karen H. Thompson 2016
41 pairs + 5 pair thinner gimp
(approximately 21 wraps/cm)
For correct size, one repeat of the pricking is
14.3 cm or 5 5/8" long

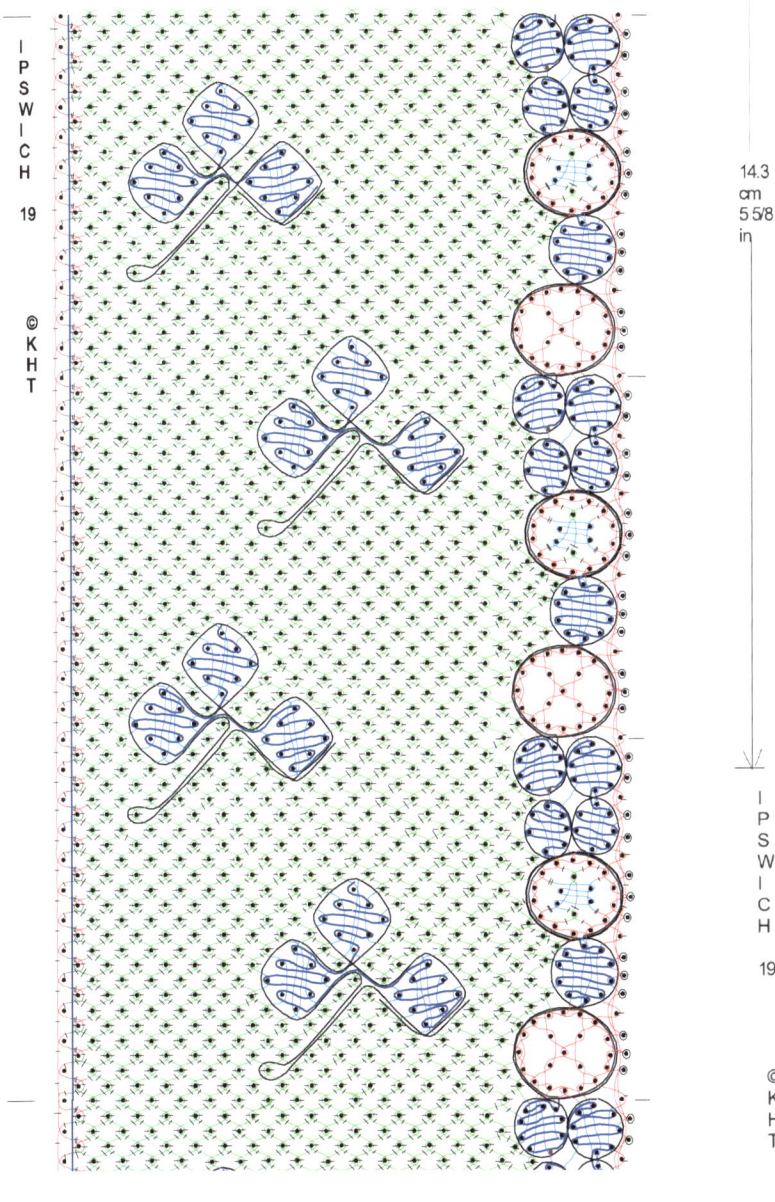

See detailed diagrams on the following 2 pages

41

IPSWICH #19 reproduction by Karen H. Thompson, Details of working diagram

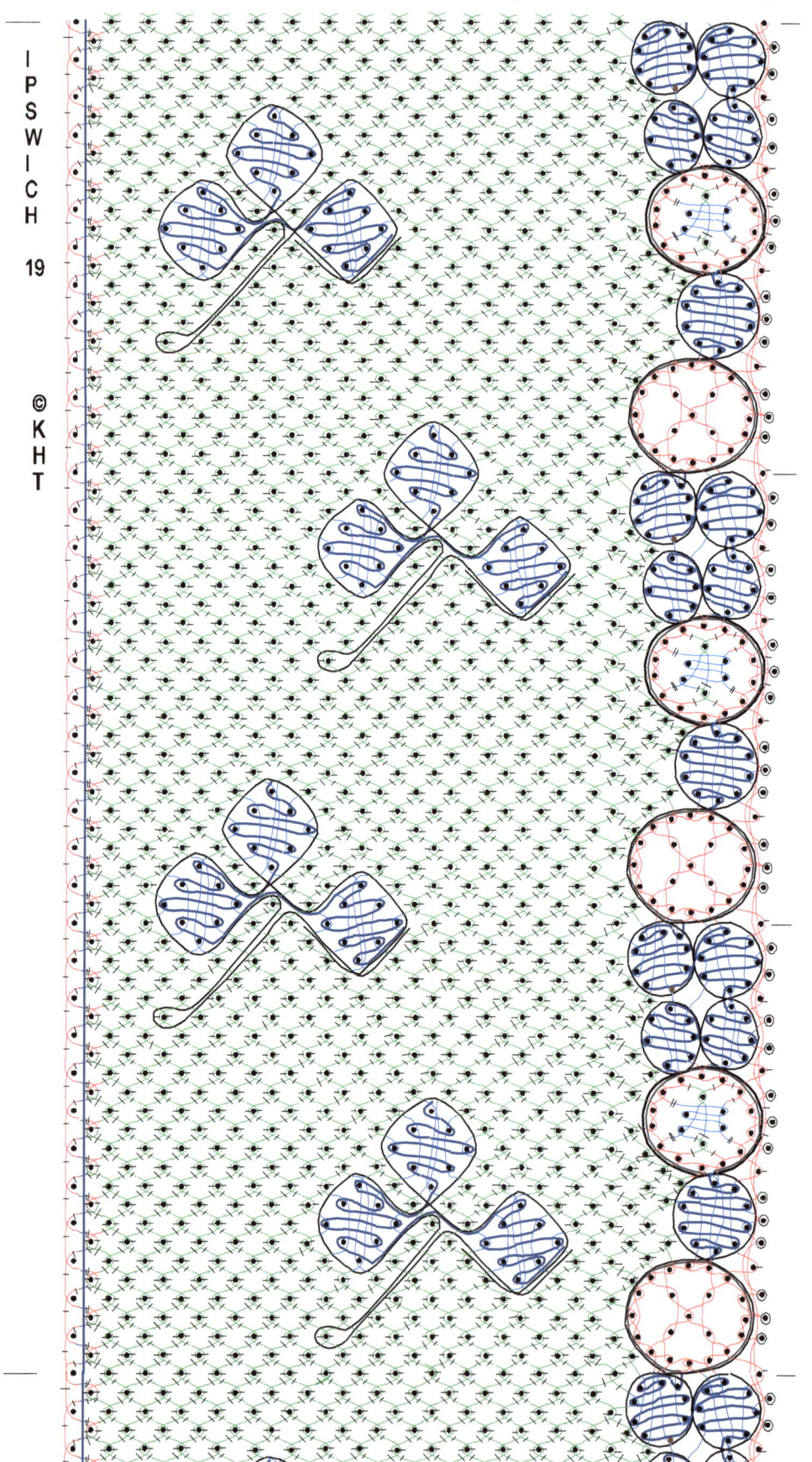

IPSWICH #19 reproduction by Karen H. Thompson, Details of working diagram

Detail of first motif

Detail of head side

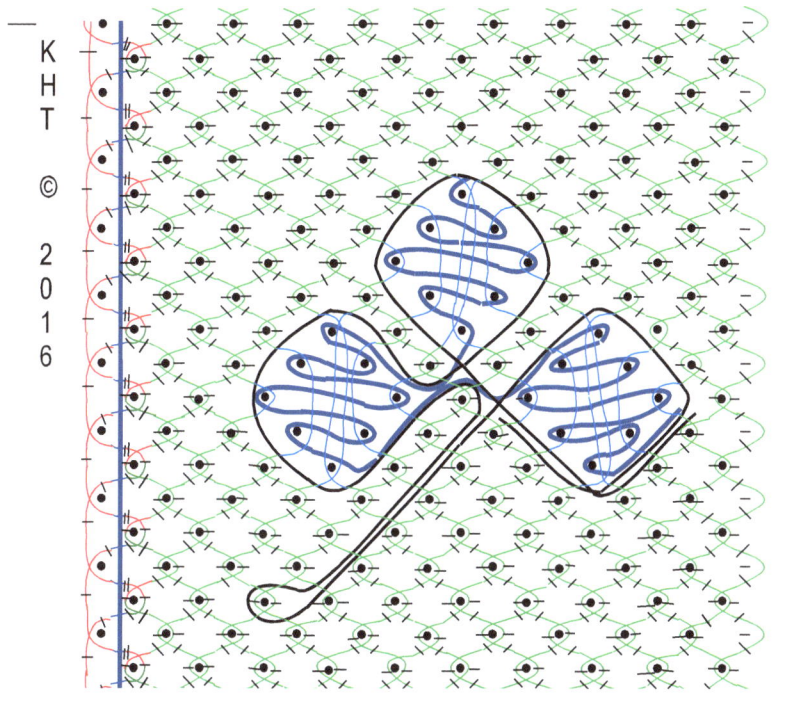

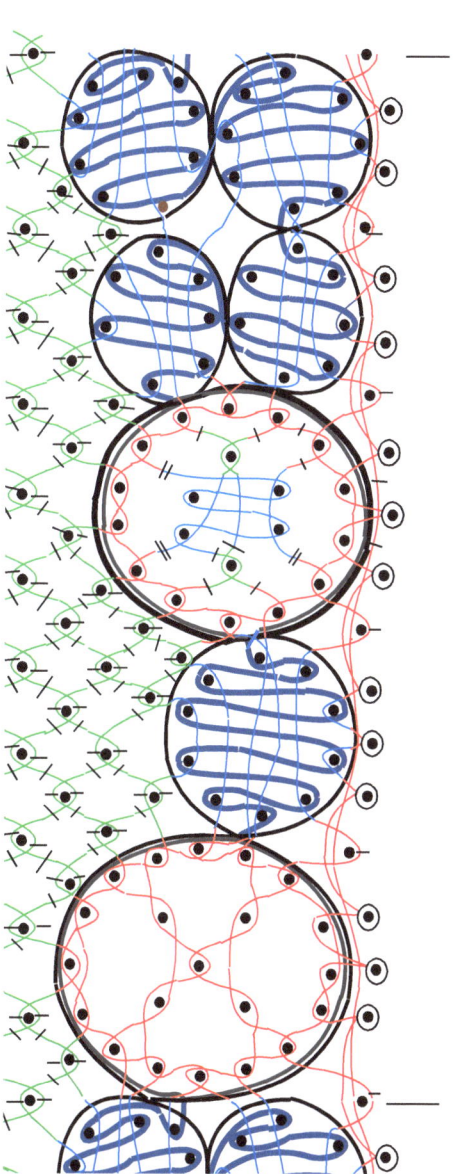

from gimp as worker to passive or opposite: work the 4 gimp threads together with linen stitch:

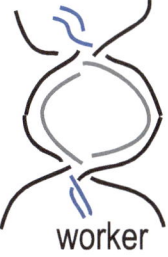

IPSWICH sample #1 made in Ipswich 1789-1790
Size of original sample:
4.4 cm (1.7") wide, 7 cm (2.8") long

Original sample

IPSWICH #1 reproduction
Width of lace is 4.4 cm (1.7")
one repeat is 2.9 cm (1 ⅛") long

Reproduction

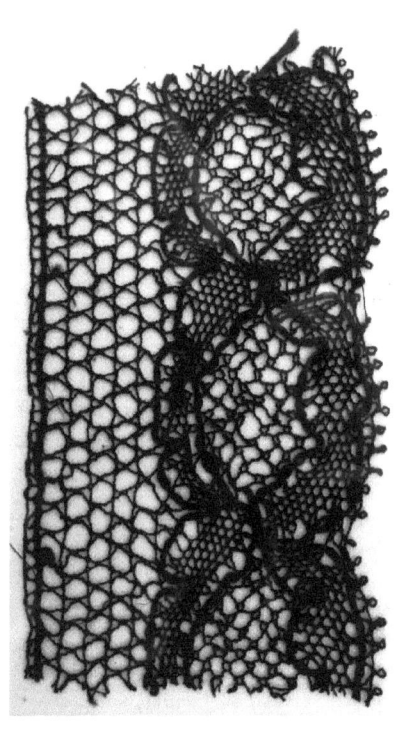
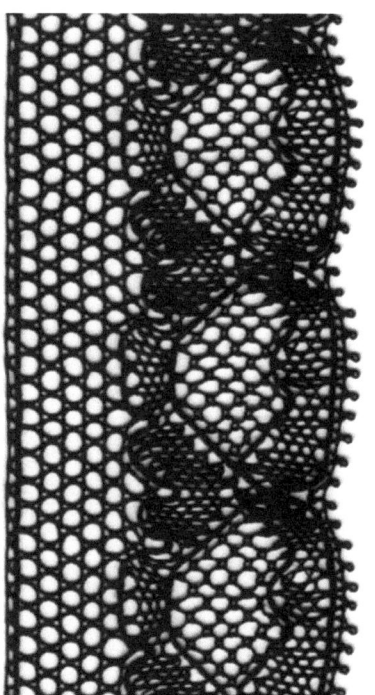

44

IPSWICH sample #1 made in Ipswich 1789-1790
Reconstructed sample by Karen H. Thompson, 2016
27 pairs + 5 single gimp threads
For correct size, one repeat of the pricking is
2.9 cm or 1 ⅛" inches long

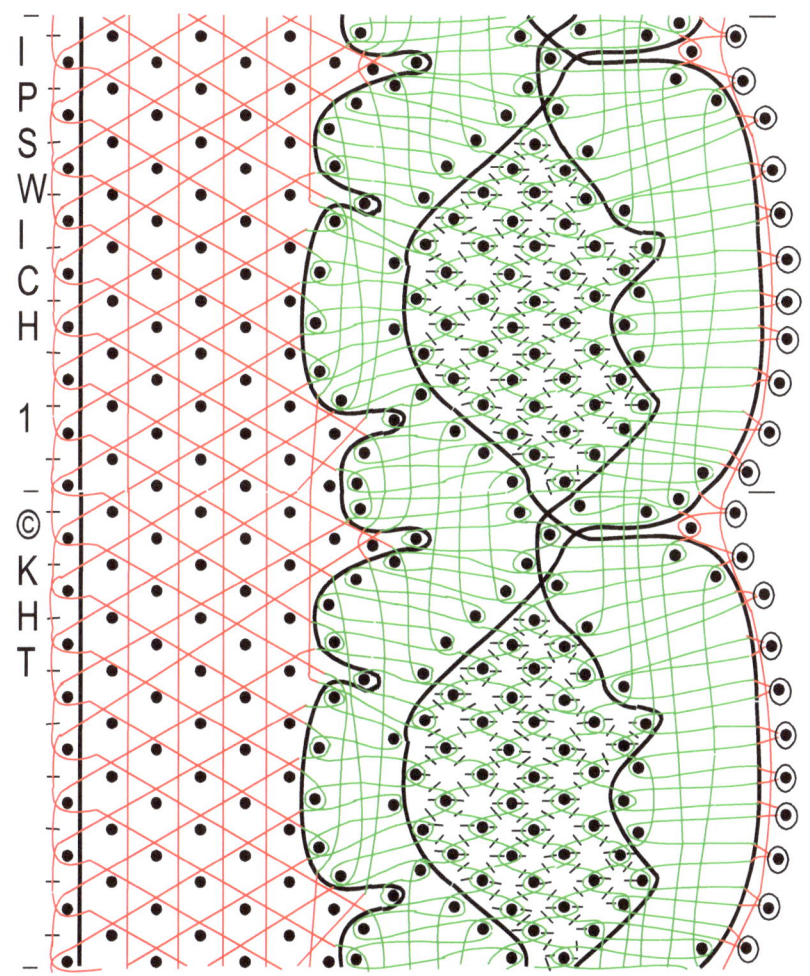
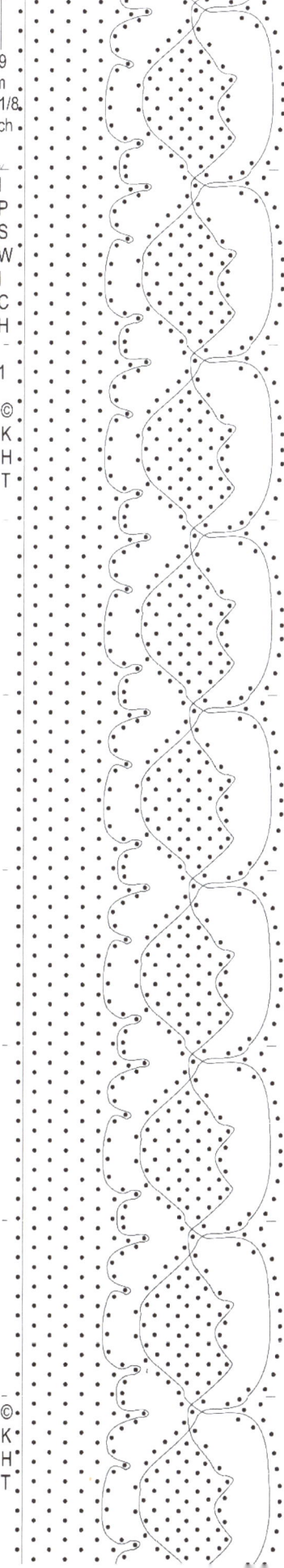

45

IPSWICH sample #6 made in Ipswich 1789-1790
Size of original sample:
5.2 cm (2") wide, 8.3 cm (3.3") long

Original sample (incomplete pattern repeat)

IPSWICH #6 reproduction
Width of lace is 5.2 cm (2")
one repeat is 14.7 cm (5 ¾") long

Lace inspired by sample with incomplete
Pattern repeat

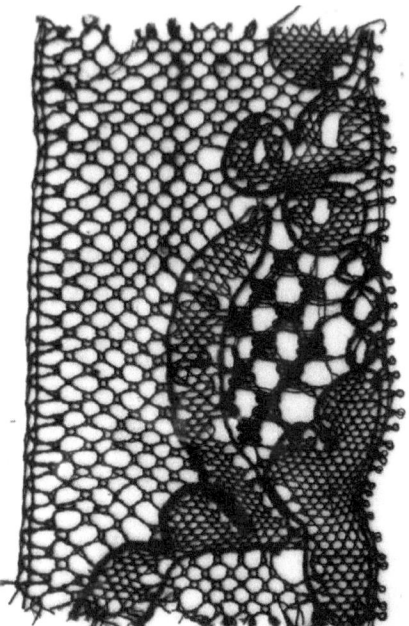
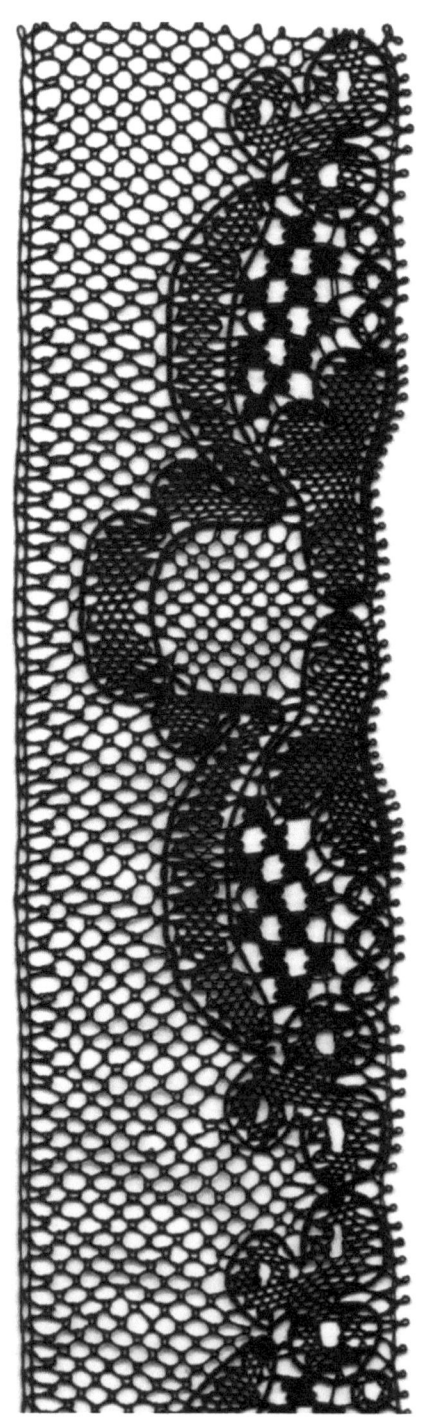

IPSWICH sample #6 made in Ipswich 1789-1790
Reconstructed sample by Karen H. Thompson, 2015
Inspired by the incomplete sample
28 pairs + 2 pair gimp threads
For correct size, one repeat of the pricking is
14.7 cm or 5 ¾" inches long

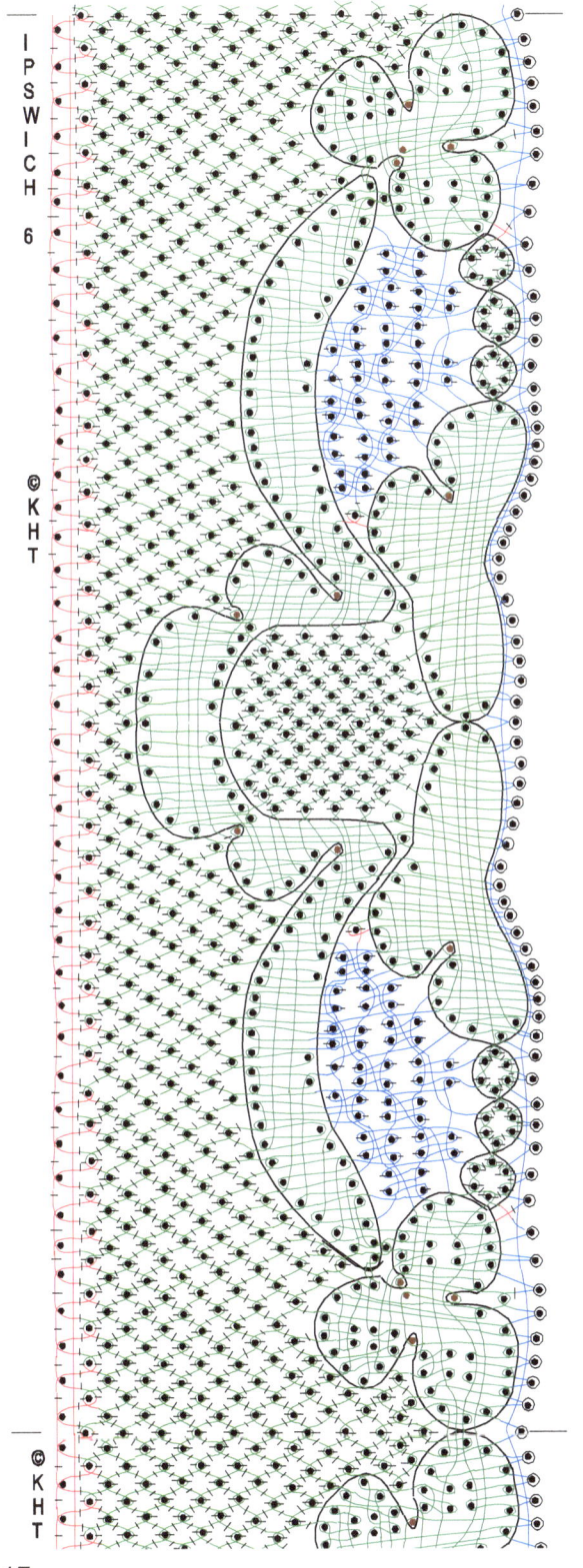
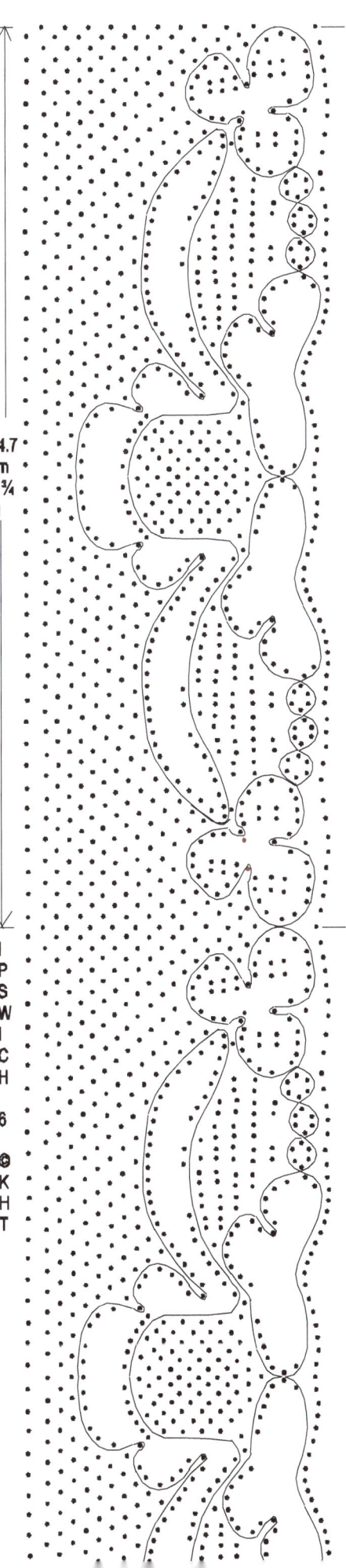

IPSWICH sample #13 made in Ipswich 1789-1790
Size of original sample, incomplete pattern repeat:
6.7 cm (2.6") wide, 7.5 cm (3") long

IPSWICH #13 reproduction
Width of lace is 6.6 cm (2.6")
one repeat is 17.3 cm (6 ¾") long

Original sample (incomplete pattern repeat)

Lace inspired by incomplete pattern repeat

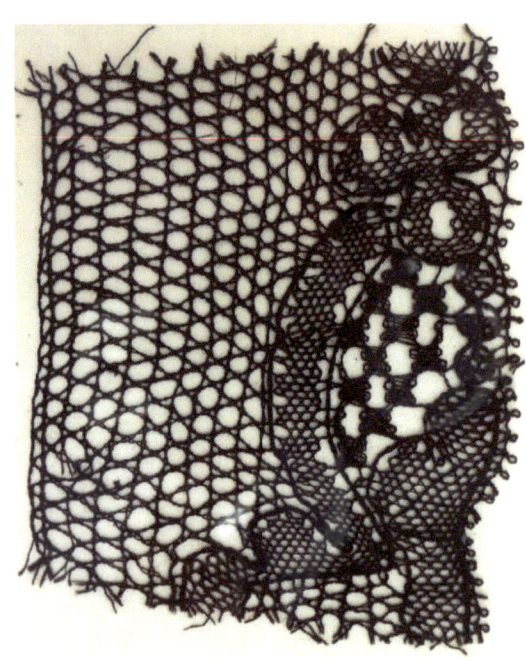
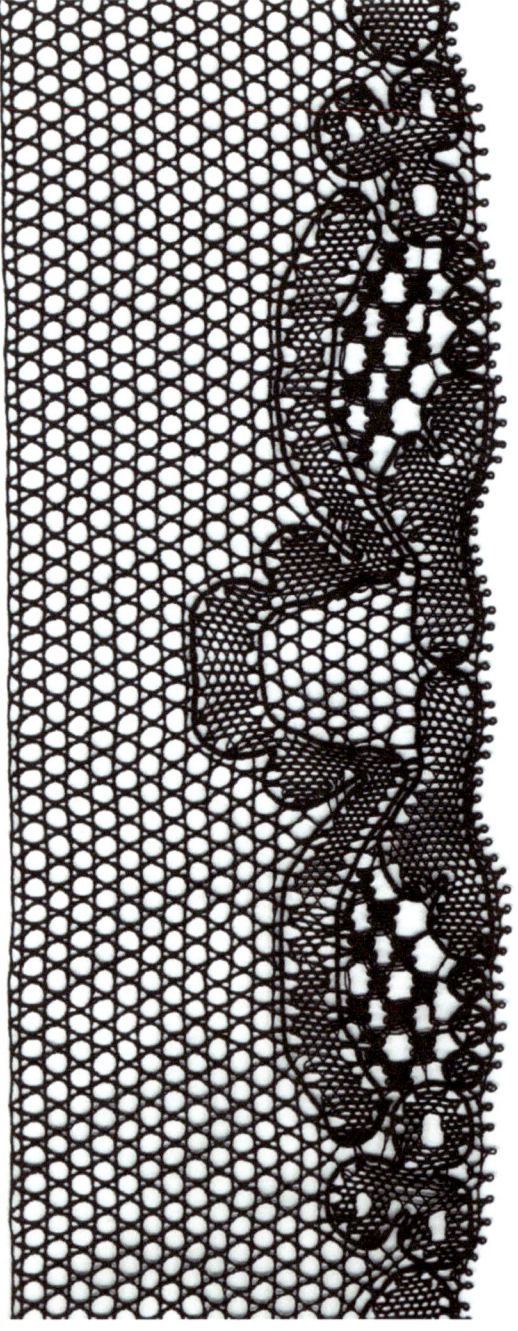

IPSWICH sample #13 made in Ipswich 1789-1790

Reconstructed sample by Karen H. Thompson, 2016

42 pairs + 2 pair gimp

For correct size, one repeat of the pricking is

17.3 cm or 6 ¾" long

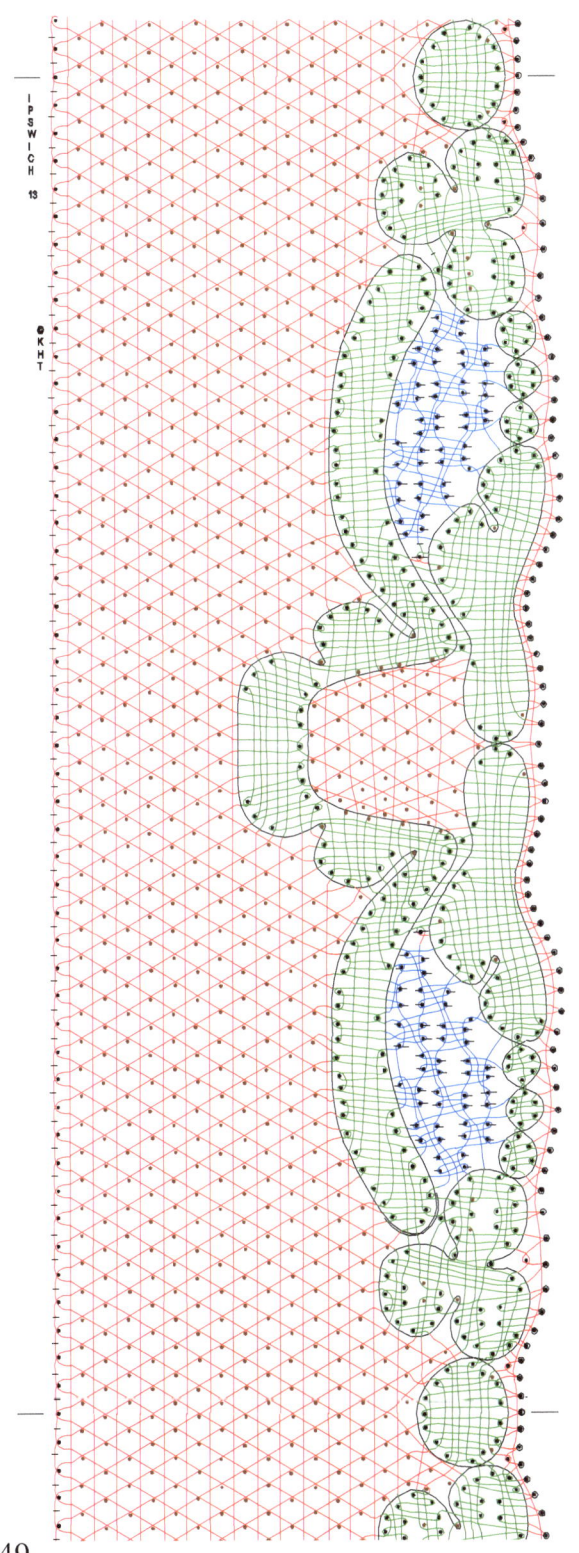
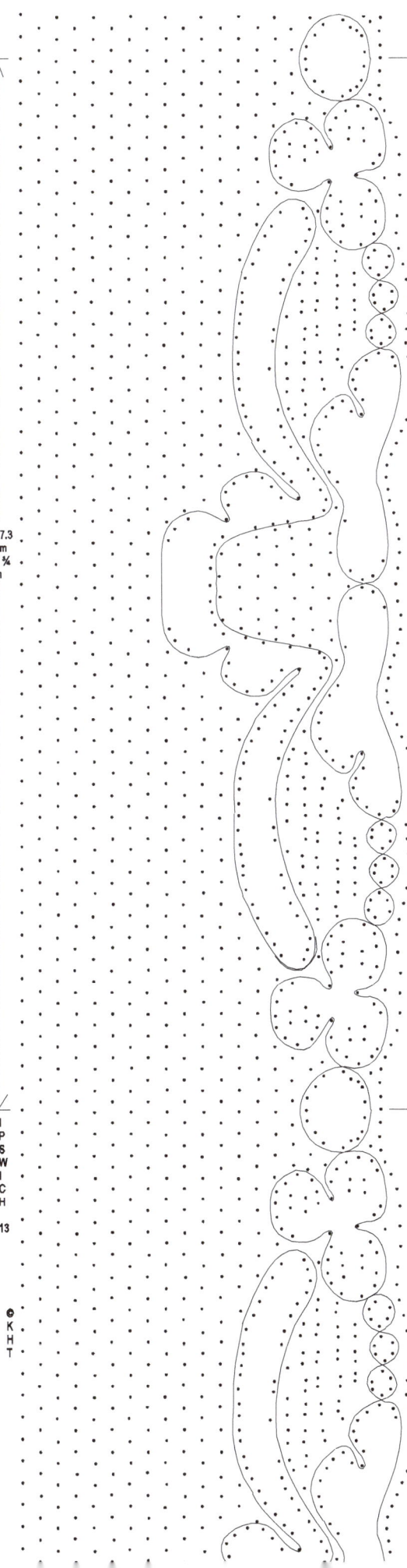

IPSWICH sample #3 made in Ipswich 1789-1790
Size of original sample:
4.8 cm (1.9") wide, 8.5 cm (3.4") long

Original sample

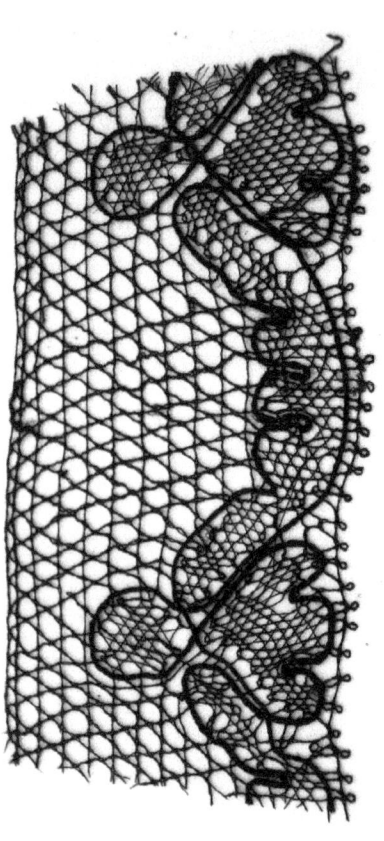

IPSWICH #3 reproduction
Width of lace is 4.7 cm (1.9")
one repeat is 5.3 cm (2 1/8") long

Reproduction

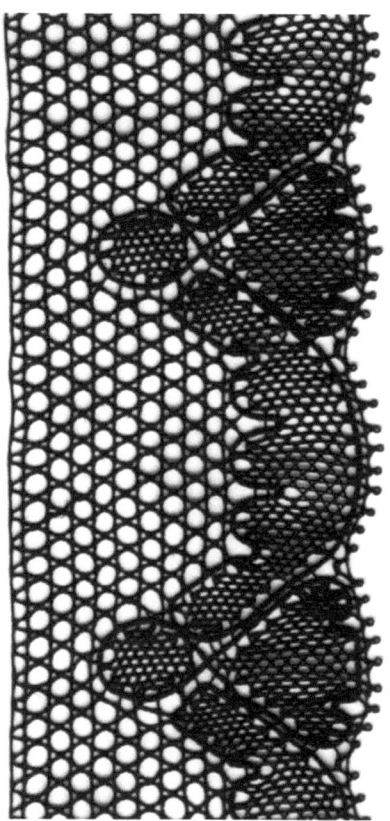

IPSWICH sample #3 made in Ipswich 1789-1790
Reconstructed sample by Karen H. Thompson, 2015
30 pairs + 2 single gimp threads
For correct size, one repeat of the pricking is
5.3 cm or 2 1/8" long

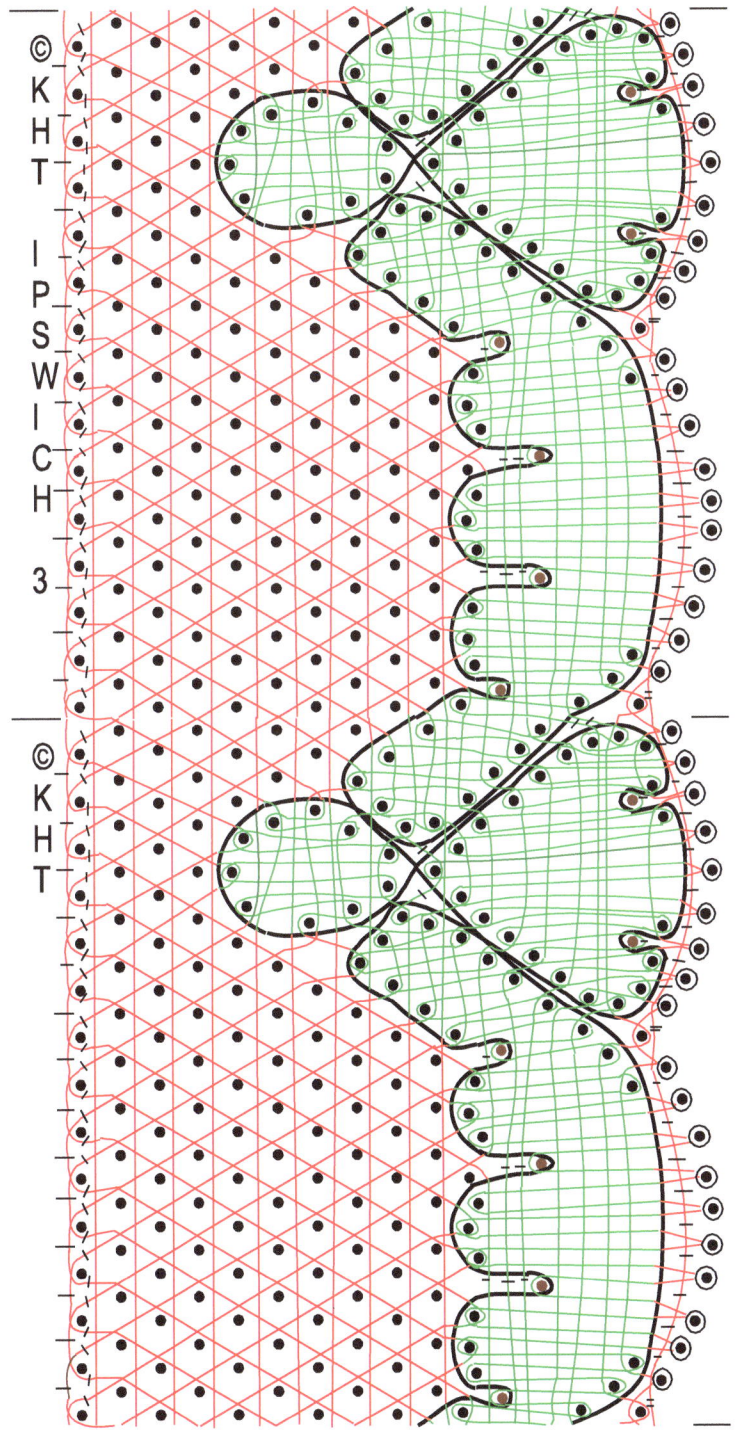
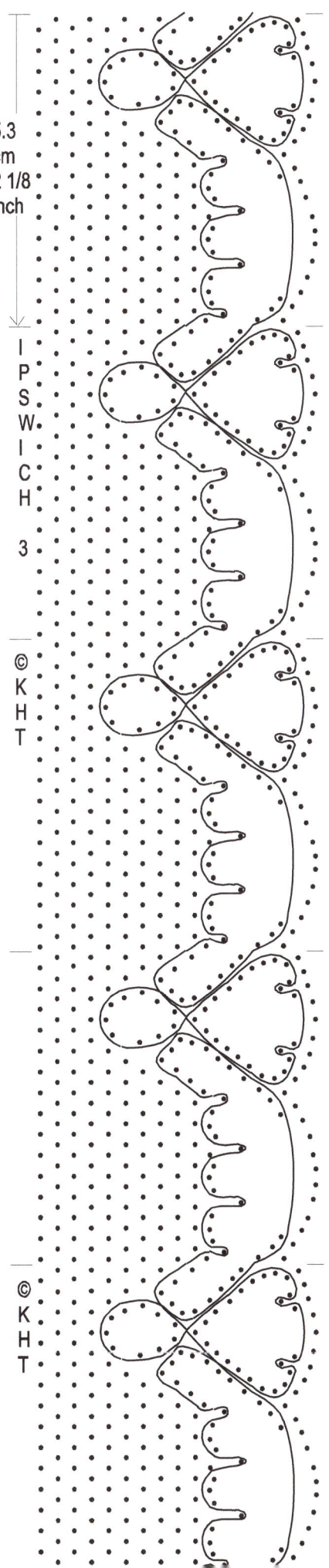

IPSWICH sample #9 made in Ipswich 1789-1790
Size of original sample:
5 cm (2") wide, 15cm (5.9") long

Original sample

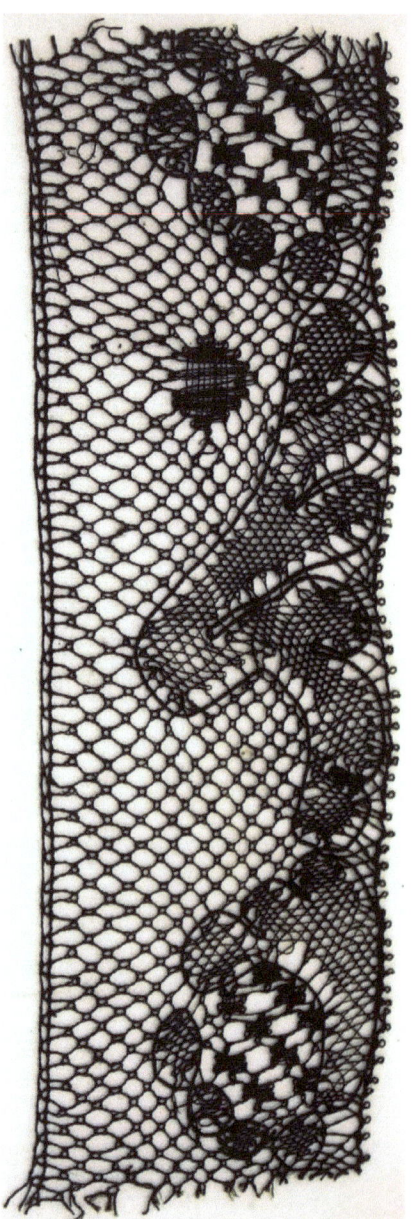

IPSWICH #9 reproduction
Width of lace is 5 cm (2")
one repeat is 12.7 cm (5") long

Reproduction

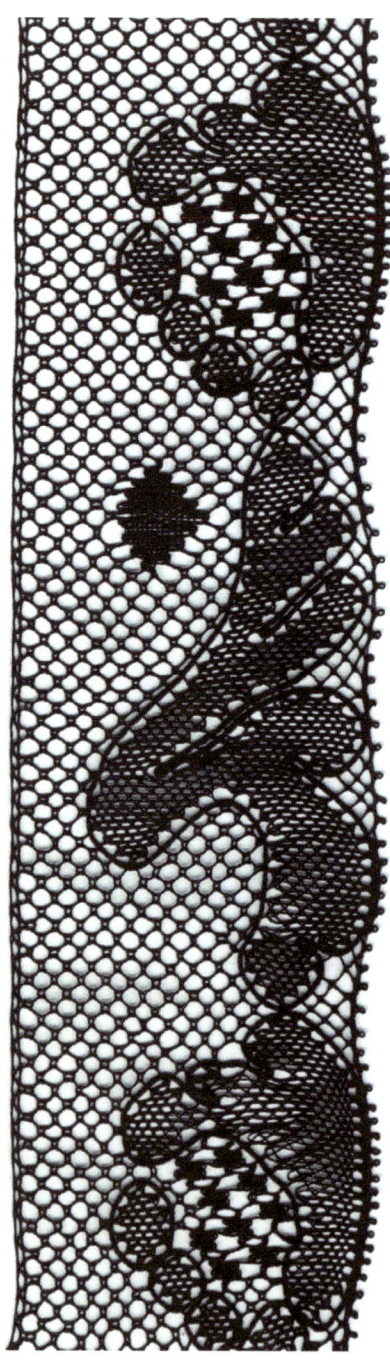

52

IPSWICH sample #9 made in Ipswich 1789-1790
Reconstructed sample by Karen H. Thompson, 2016
31 pairs + 2 pair gimp
For correct size, one repeat of the pricking is
12.7 cm or 5" long

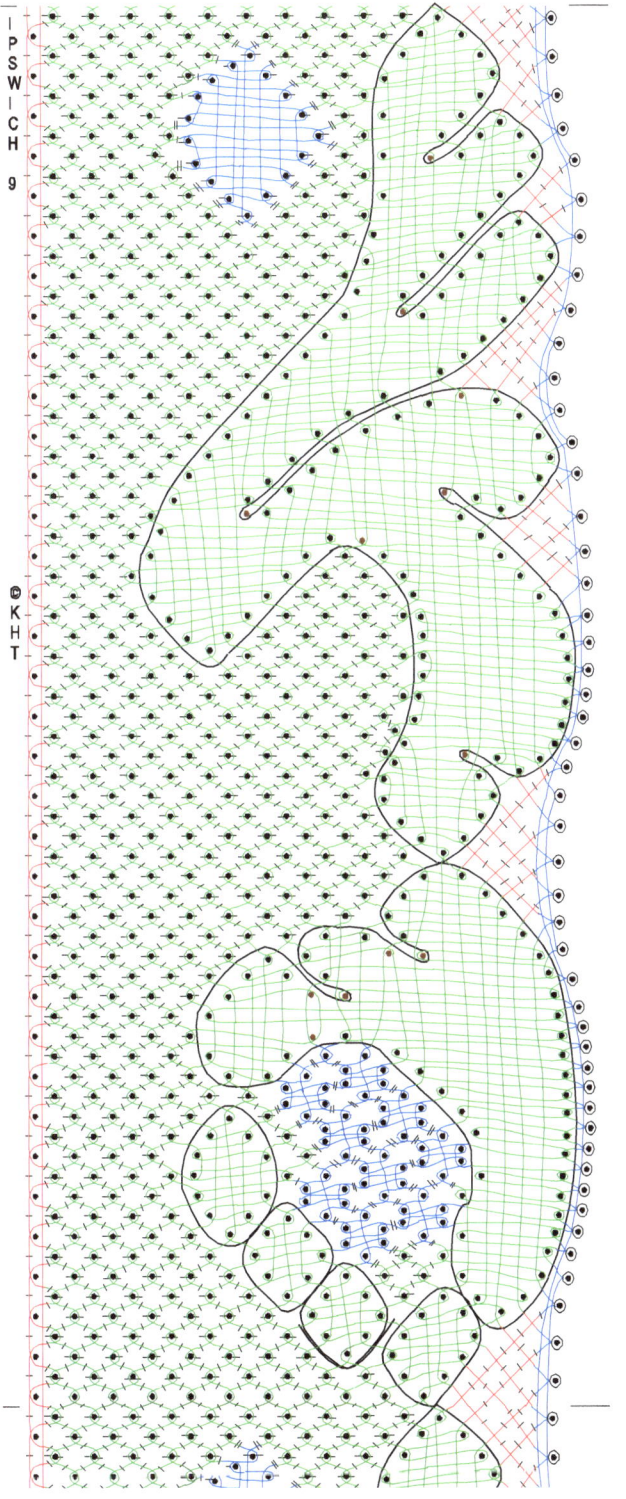
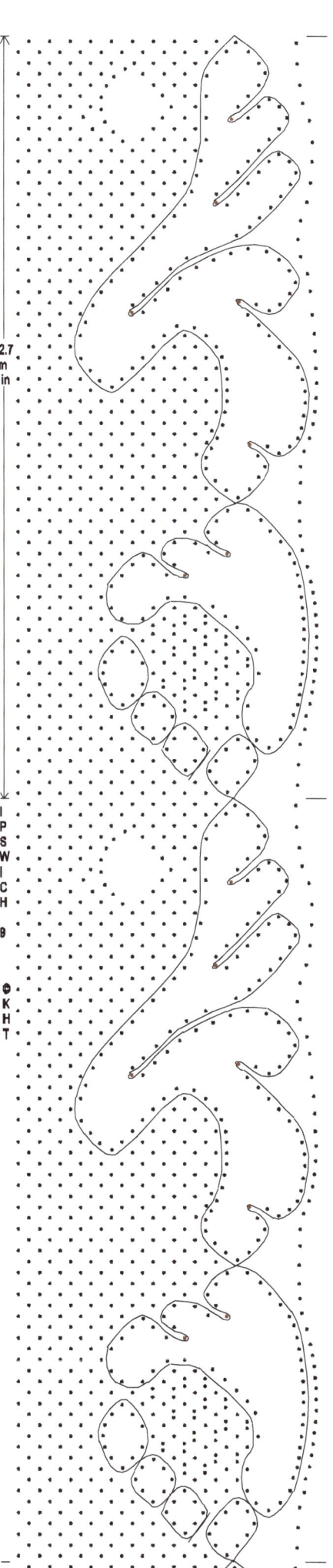

IPSWICH sample #10 made in Ipswich 1789-1790

Size of original sample:

6 cm (2.4") wide, 12cm (4.7") long

Original sample

IPSWICH #10 reproduction

Width of lace is 6 cm (2.4")

one repeat is 13.3 cm (5 ¼") long

Reproduction

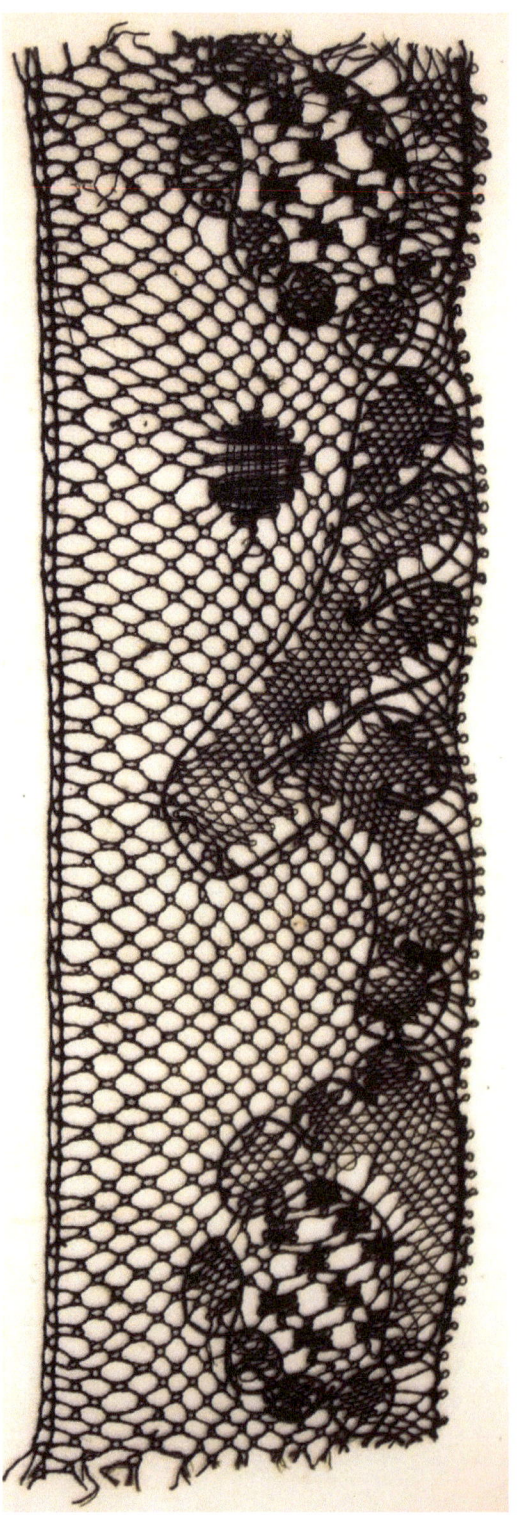

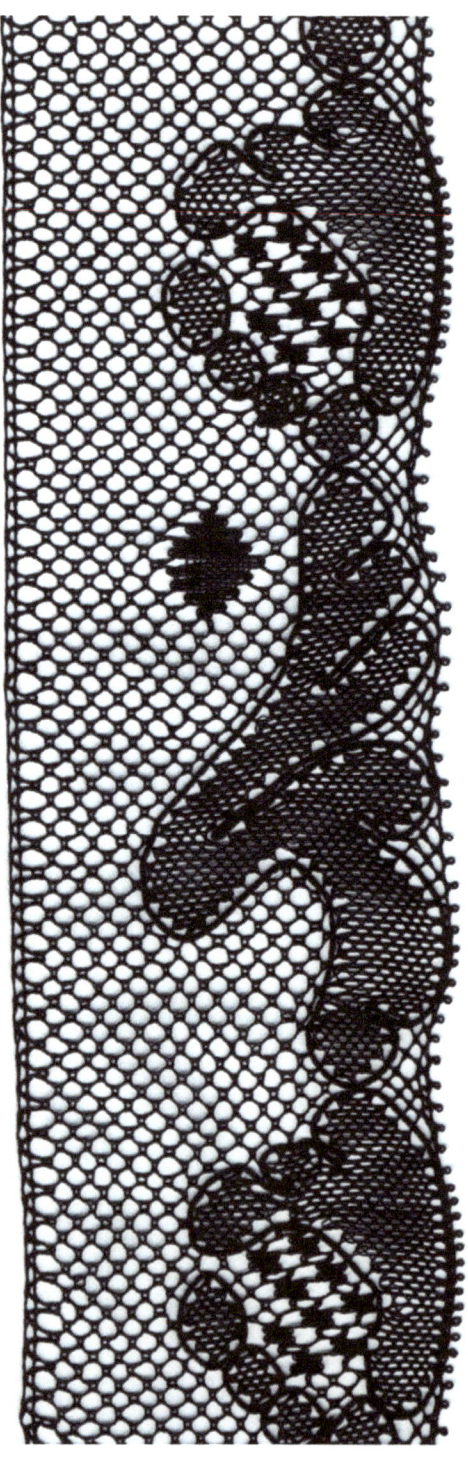

54

IPSWICH sample #10 made in Ipswich 1789-1790
Reconstructed sample by Karen H. Thompson, 2016
34 pairs + 2 pair gimp
For correct size, one repeat of the pricking is
13.3 cm or 5 ¼" long

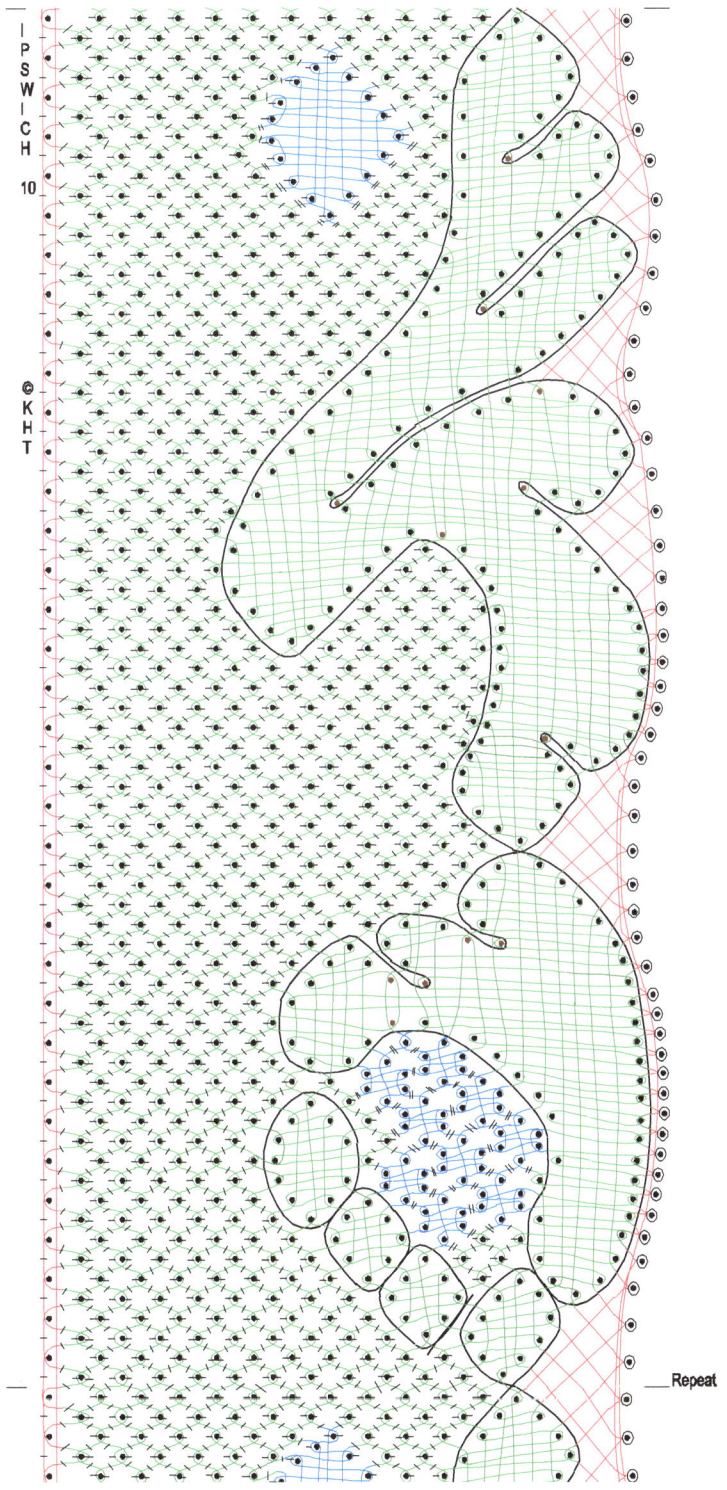
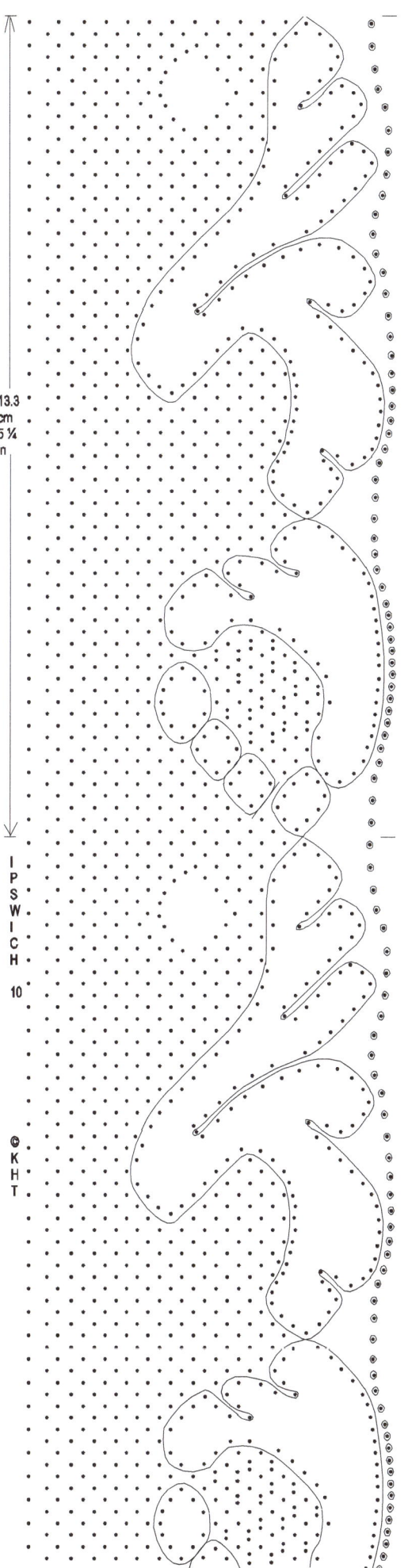

IPSWICH sample #4 made in Ipswich 1789-1790
Size of original sample:
5 cm (2") wide, 9 cm (3.5") long

IPSWICH #4 reproduction
Width of lace is 5 cm (2")
one repeat is 7.7 cm (3") long

Original sample

Reproduction

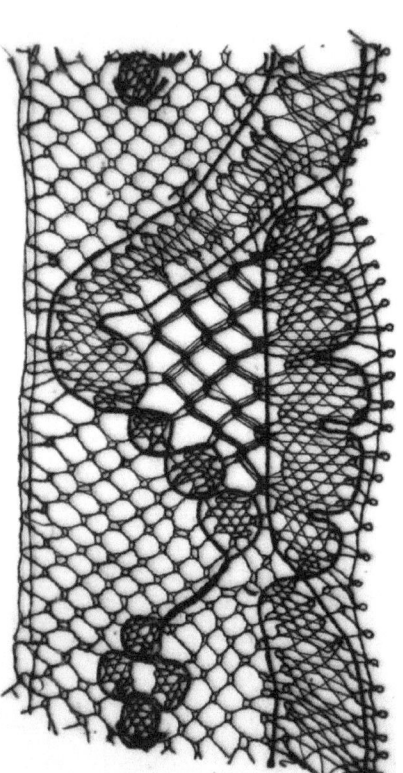
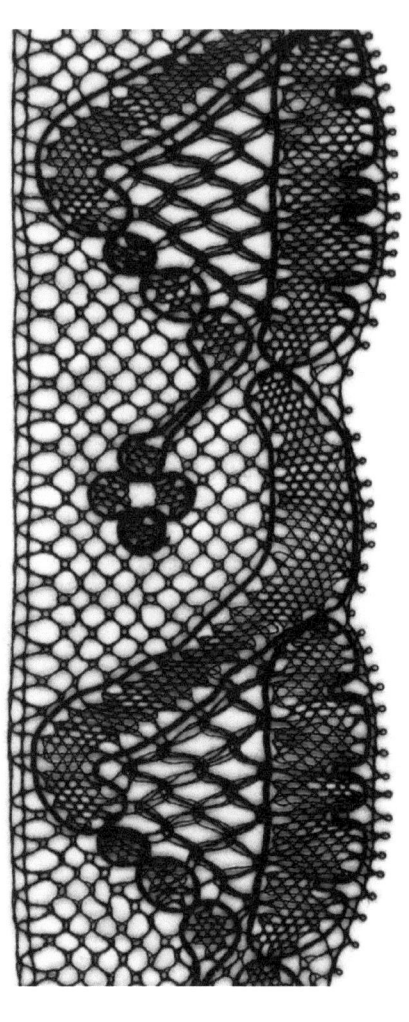

IPSWICH sample #4 made in Ipswich 1789-1790
Reconstructed sample by Karen H. Thompson, 2015
25 pairs + 2 pairs gimp threads
For correct size, one repeat of the pricking is
7.7 cm or 3" long

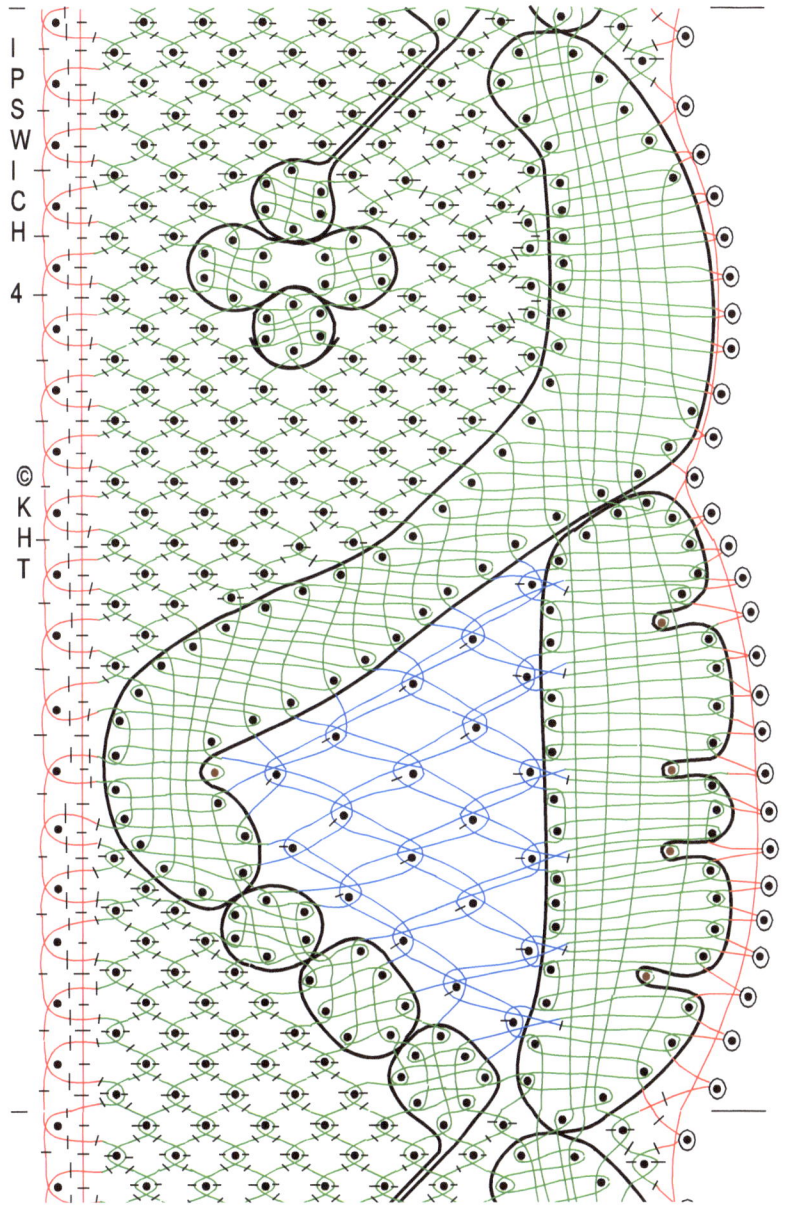
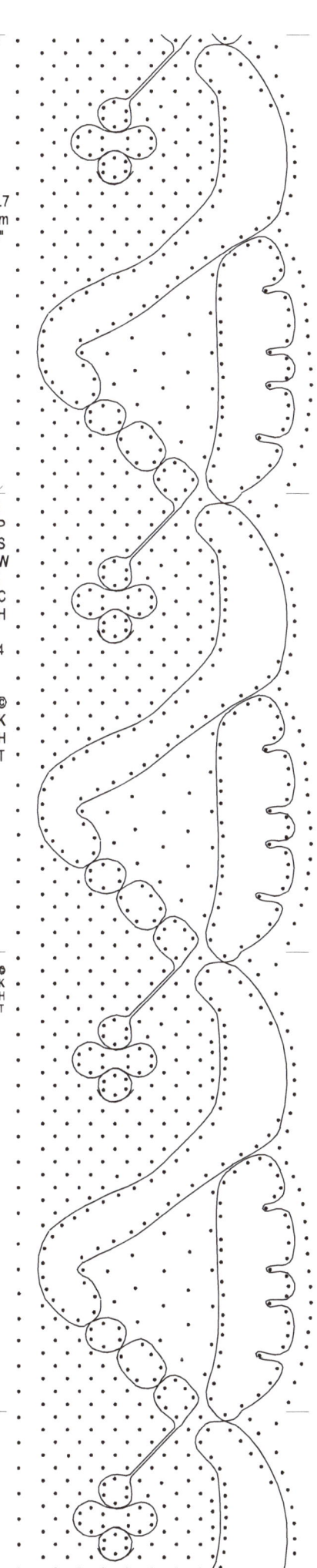

57

IPSWICH sample #15 made in Ipswich 1789-1790
Size of original sample:
6.7 cm (2.6") wide, 16 cm (6.3") long

Original sample

IPSWICH #15 reproduction
Width of lace is 6.7 cm (2.6")
one repeat is 8.7 cm (3 7/16") long

Reproduction

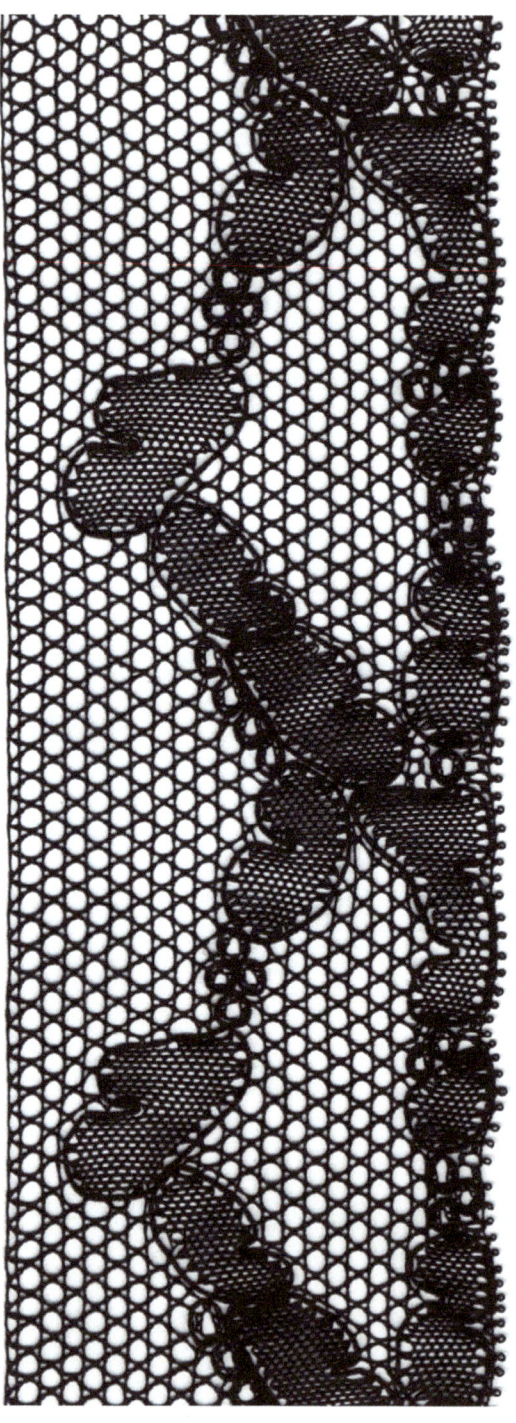

IPSWICH sample #15 made in Ipswich 1789-1790
Reconstructed sample by Karen H. Thompson, 2016
48 pairs + 2 pair gimp
For correct size, one repeat of the pricking is
8.7 cm or 3 7/16" long

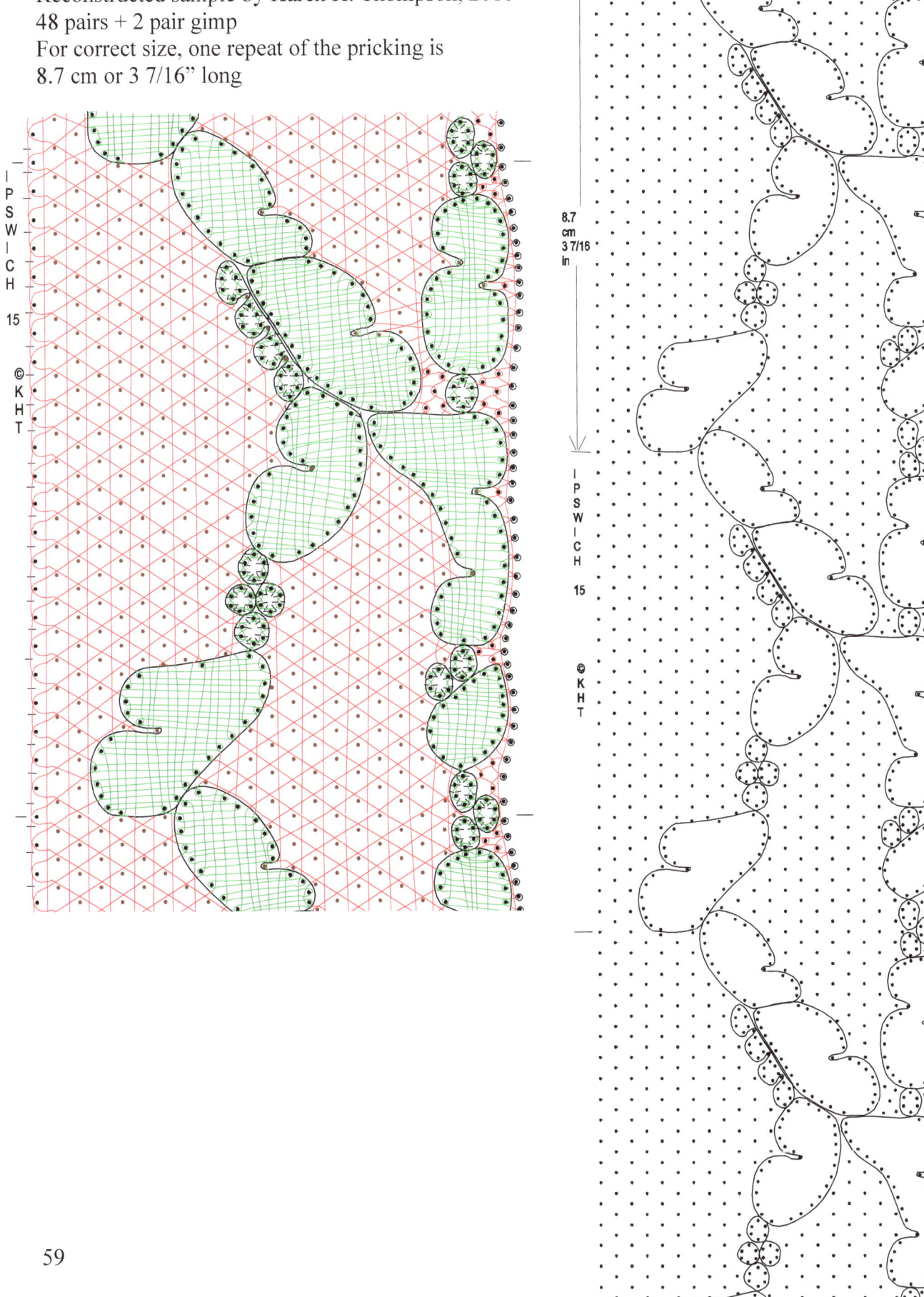

IPSWICH sample #14 made in Ipswich 1789-1790
Size of original sample:
6.3 cm (2.5") wide, 14 cm (5.5") long

IPSWICH #14 reproduction
Width of lace is 6.3 cm (2.5")
one repeat is 10.2 cm (4") long

Original sample

Reproduction

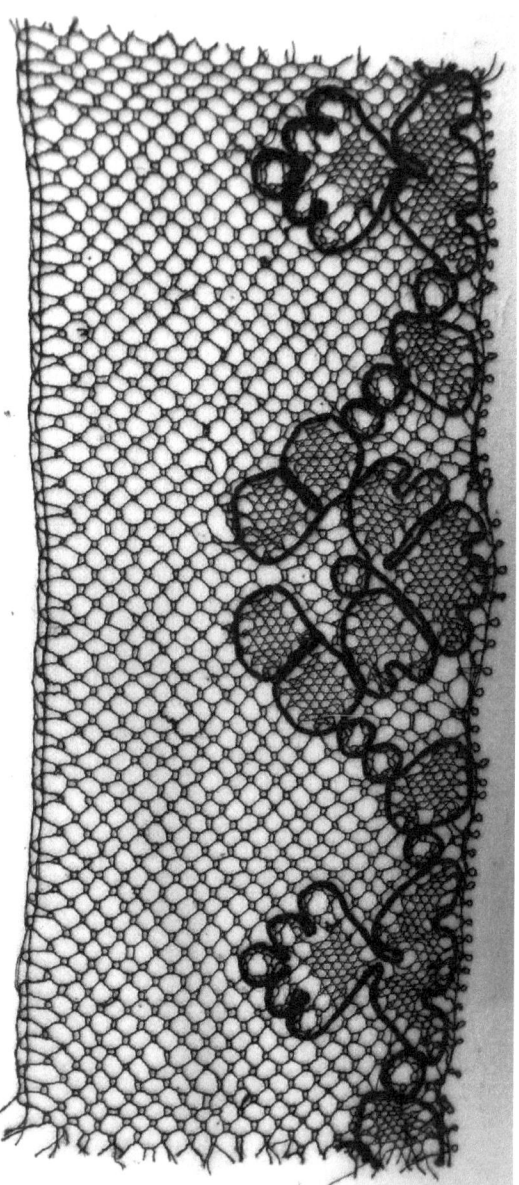
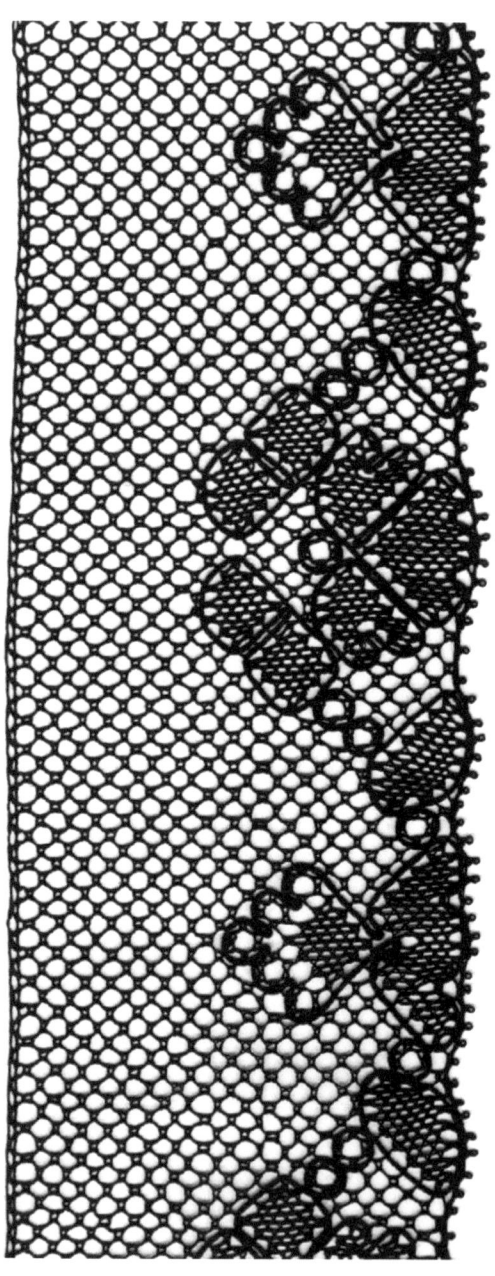

IPSWICH sample #14 made in Ipswich 1789-1790
Reconstructed sample by Karen H. Thompson, 2016
36 pairs + 1 pair gimp
For correct size, one repeat of the pricking is
10.2 cm or 4" long

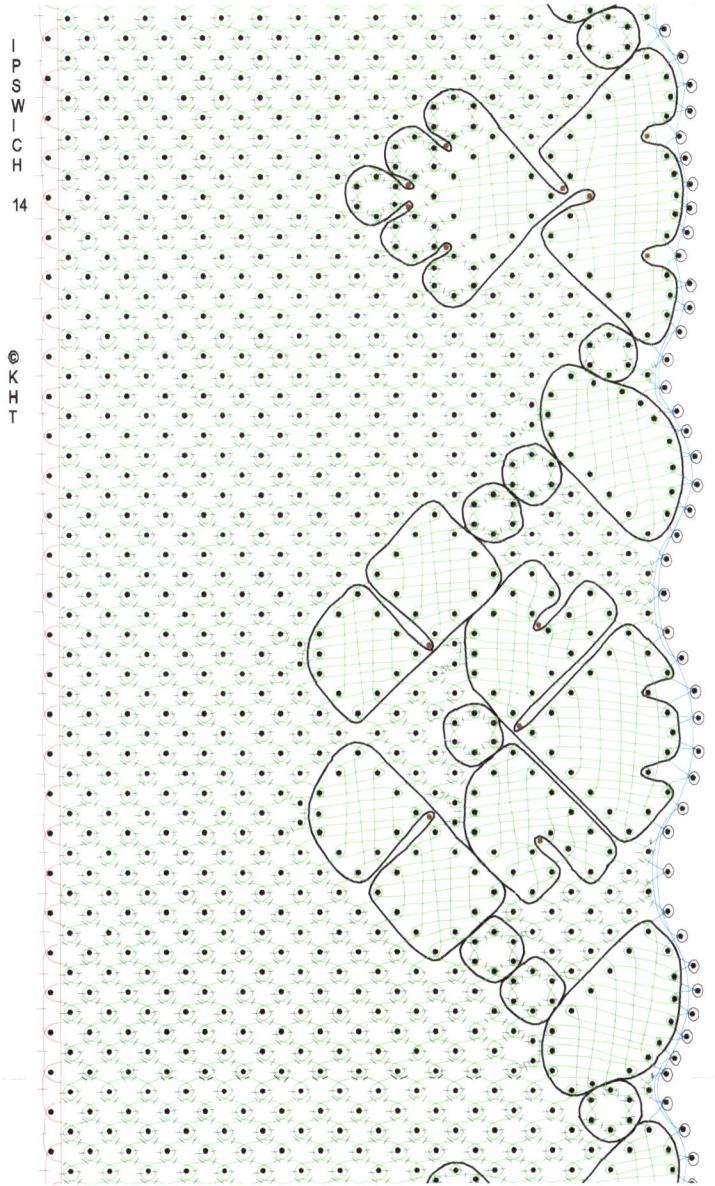

IPSWICH sample #12 made in Ipswich 1789-1790
Size of original sample:
6.6 cm (2.6") wide, 10.7cm (4.2") long

IPSWICH #12 reproduction
Width of lace is 6.6 cm (2.6")
one repeat is 9.8 cm (3 7/8") long

Original sample

Reproduction

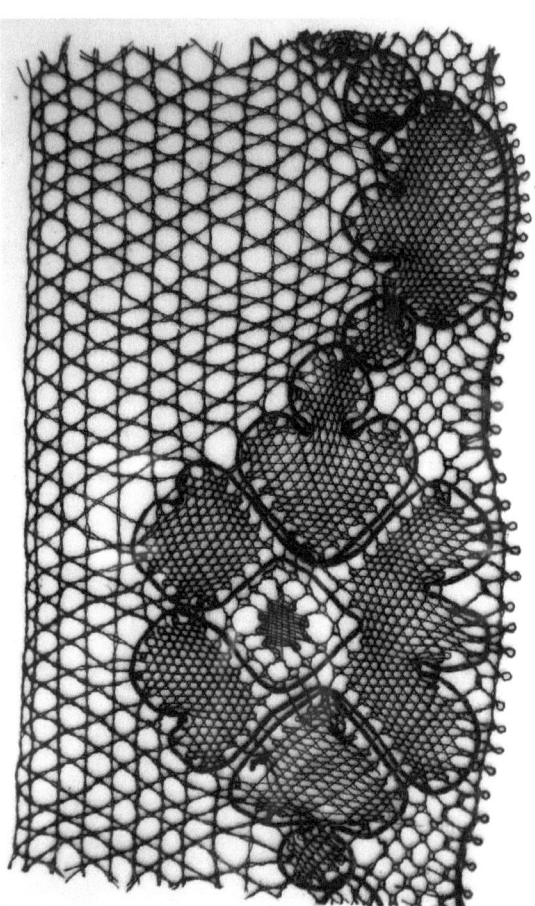
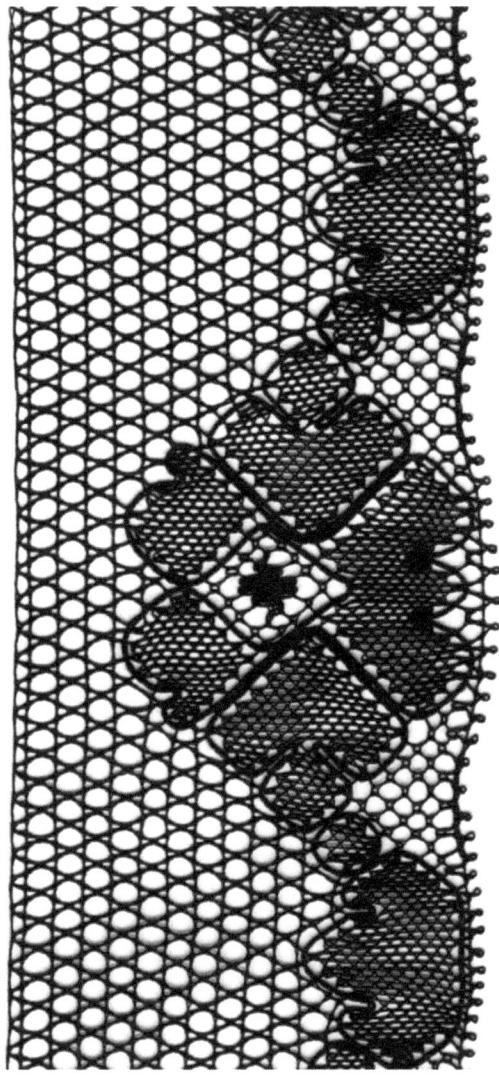

IPSWICH sample #12 made in Ipswich 1789-1790
Reconstructed sample by Karen H. Thompson, 2016
35 pairs + 1 pair gimp
For correct size, one repeat of the pricking is
9.8 cm or 3 7/8" long

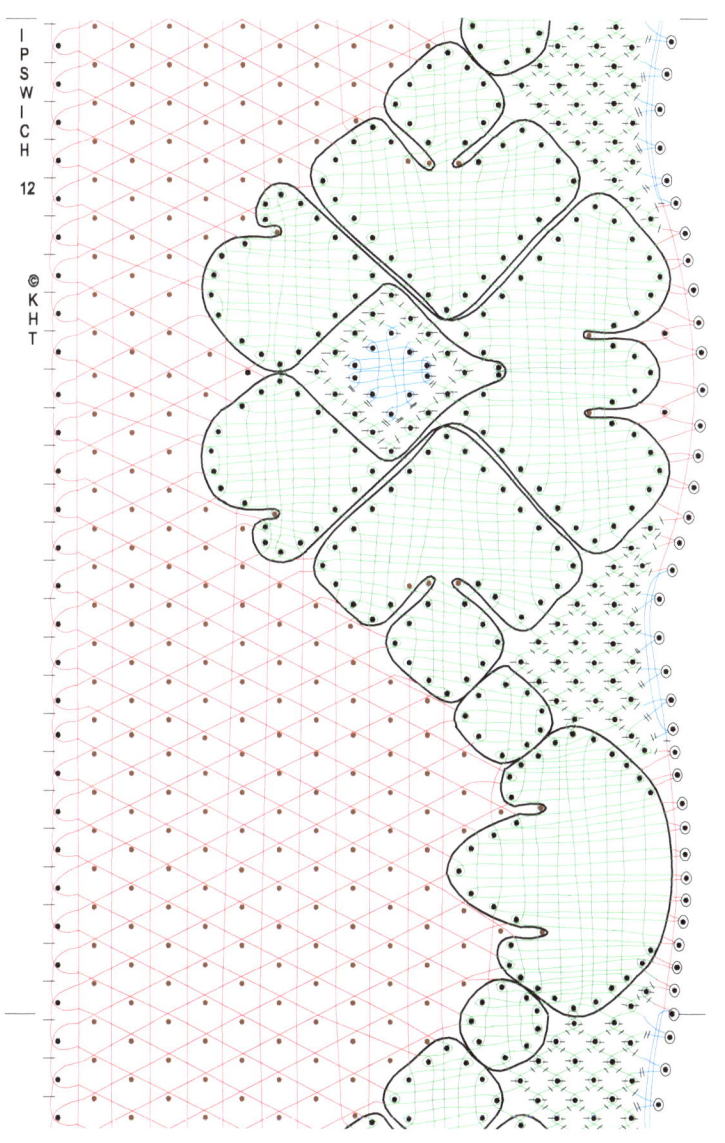
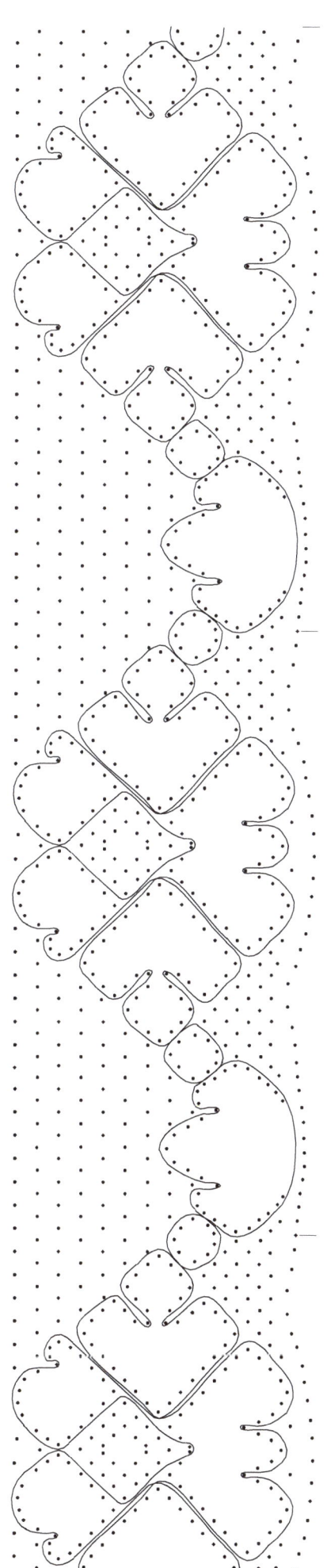

IPSWICH sample #16 made in Ipswich 1789-1790
Size of original sample:
5.7 cm (2.2") wide, 16 cm (6.3") long

IPSWICH #16 reproduction
Width of lace is 5.7 cm (2.2")
one repeat is 9.4 cm (3 ¾") long

Original sample

Reproduction

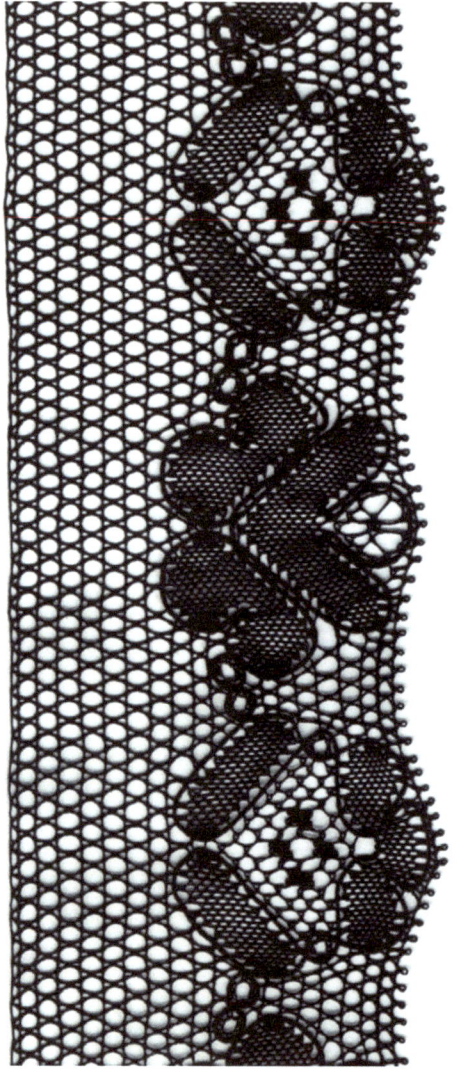

64

IPSWICH sample #16 made in Ipswich 1789-1790
Reconstructed sample by Karen H. Thompson, 2016
41 pairs + 1 pair gimp
For correct size, one repeat of the pricking is
9.4 cm or 3 ¾" long

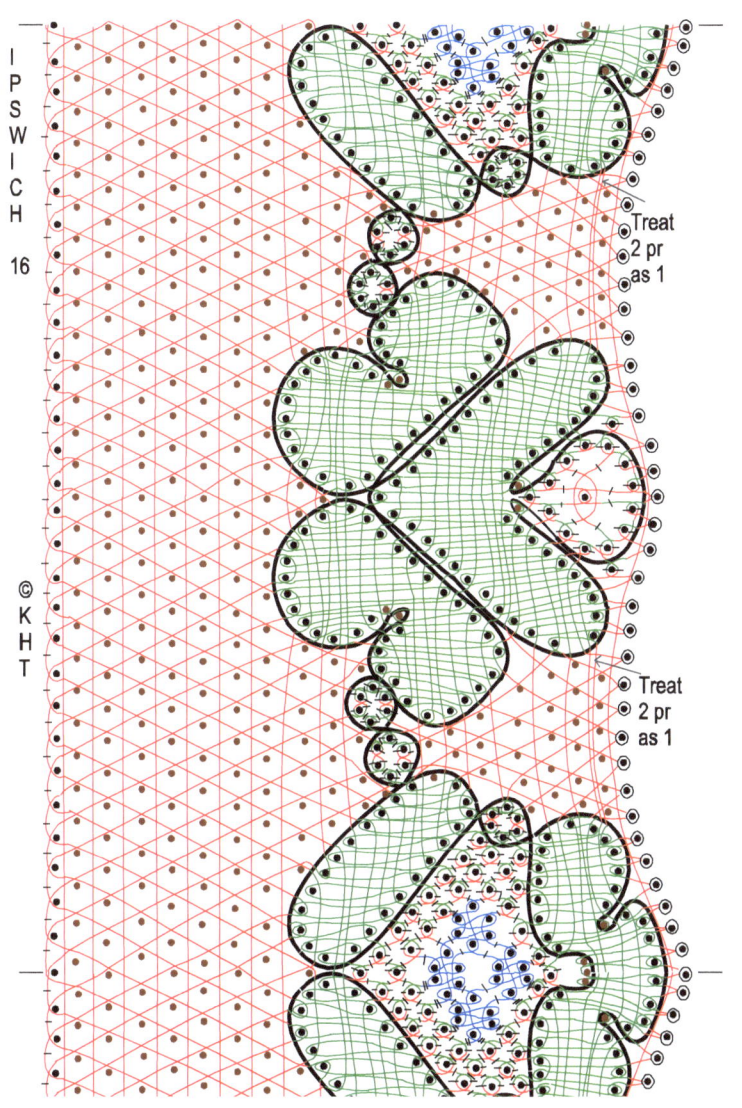
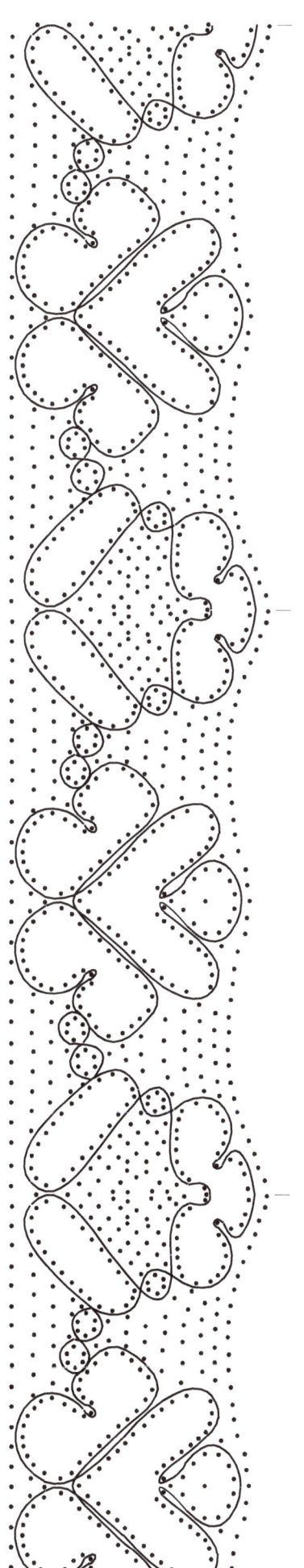

IPSWICH sample #21 made in Ipswich 1789-1790
Size of original sample:
6.7 cm (2.6") wide, 17.3 cm (6.8") long

Original sample

IPSWICH #21 reproduction
Width of lace is 6.7 cm (2.6")
one repeat is 14.6 cm (5 ¾") long

Reproduction

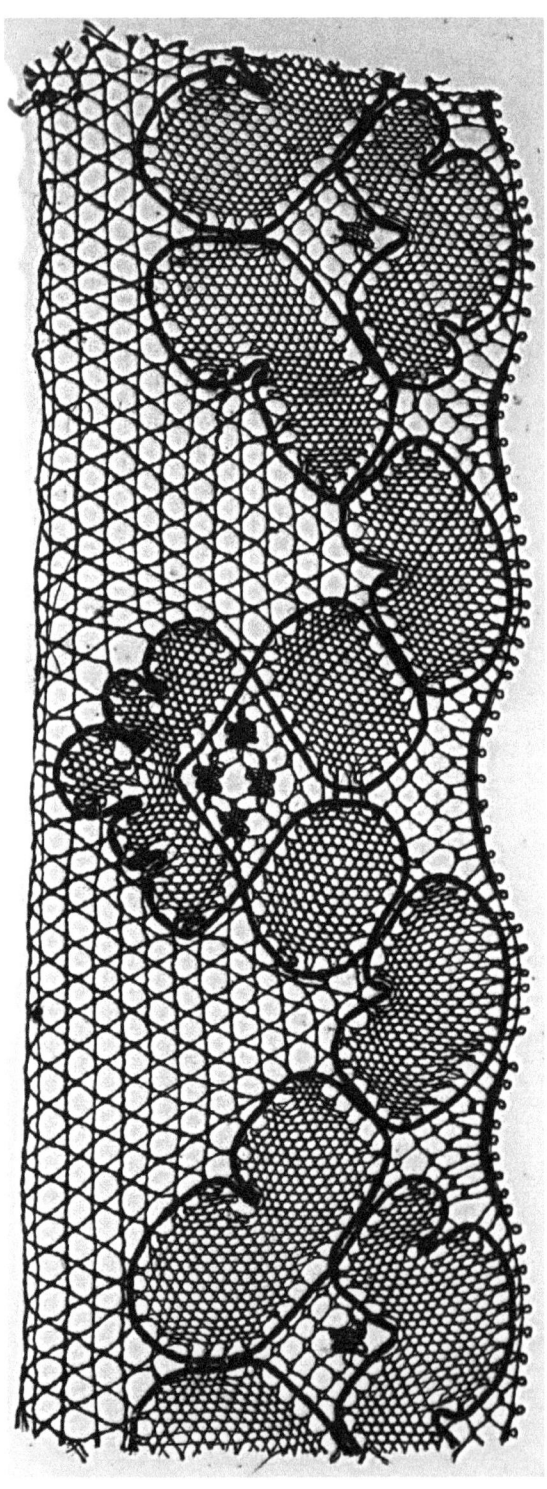
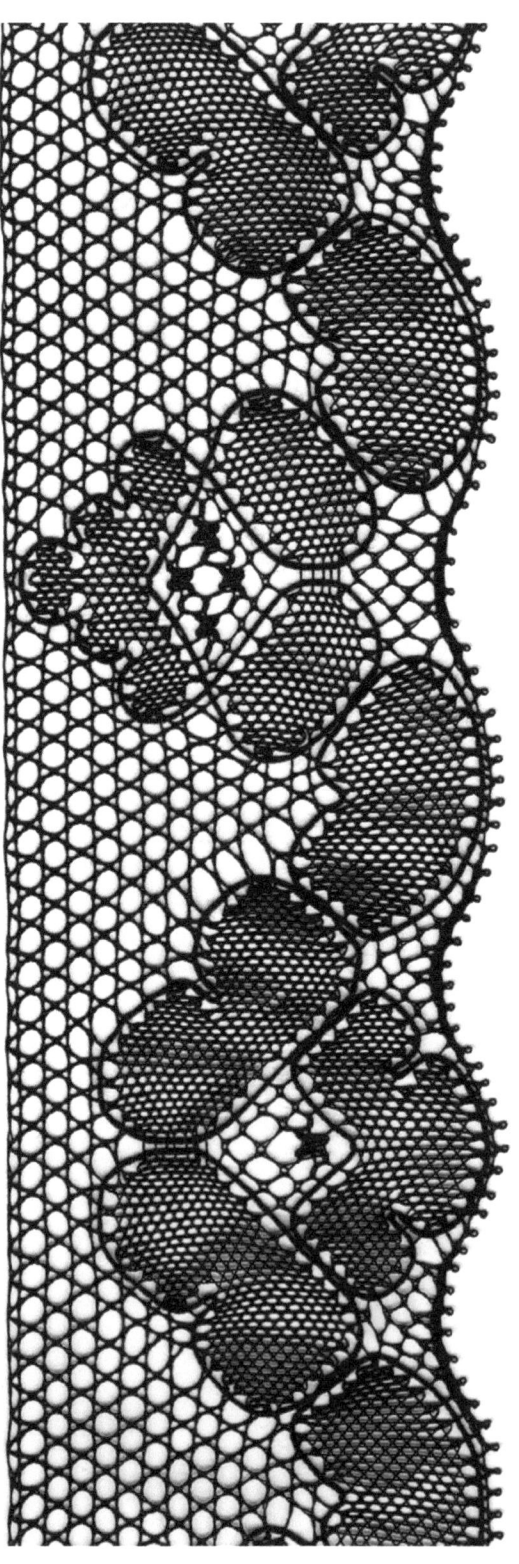

66

IPSWICH sample #21 made in Ipswich 1789-1790
Reconstructed sample by Karen H. Thompson, 2016
38 pairs + 2 single gimp threads
For correct size, one repeat of the pricking is
14.6 cm or 5 ¾" long

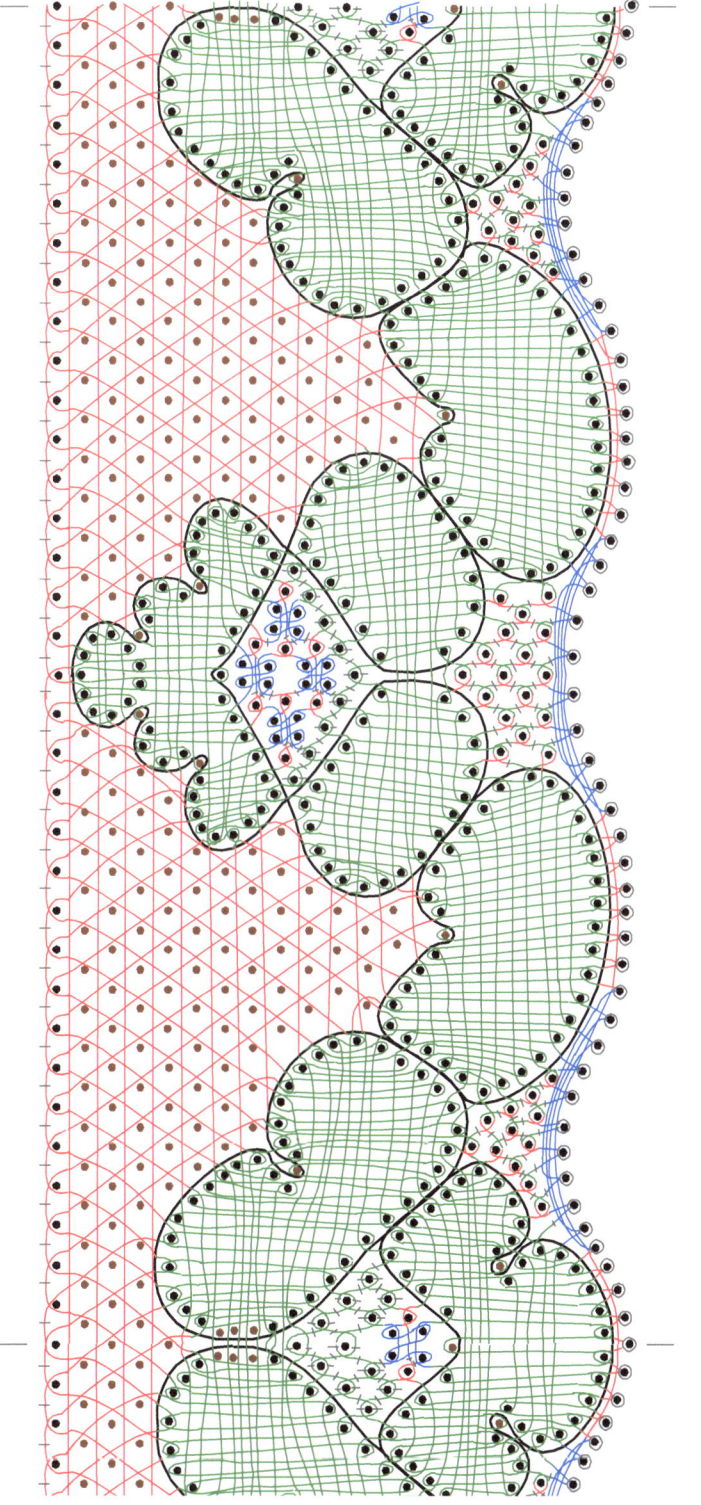

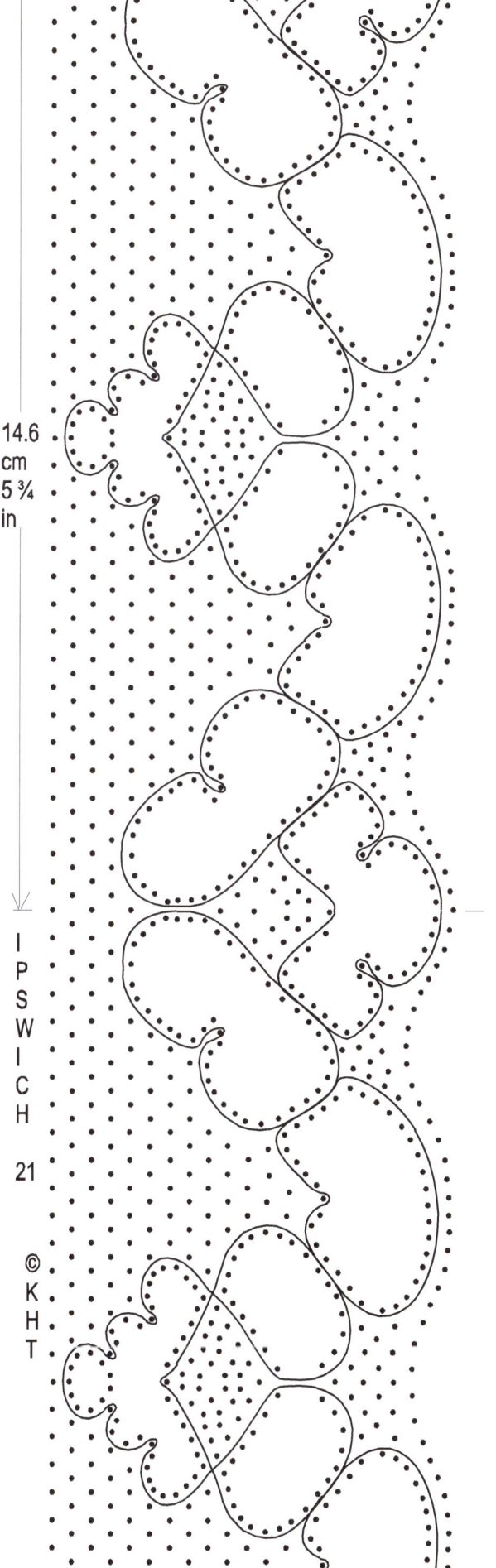

14.6 cm
5 ¾ in

IPSWICH 21
© KHT

67

IPSWICH sample #22 made in Ipswich 1789-1790
Size of original sample:
5.2 cm (2") wide, 22 cm (8.7") long
long
Original sample

IPSWICH #22 reproduction
Width of lace is 5.2 cm (2")
one repeat is 22.1 cm (8 11/16")

Reproduction

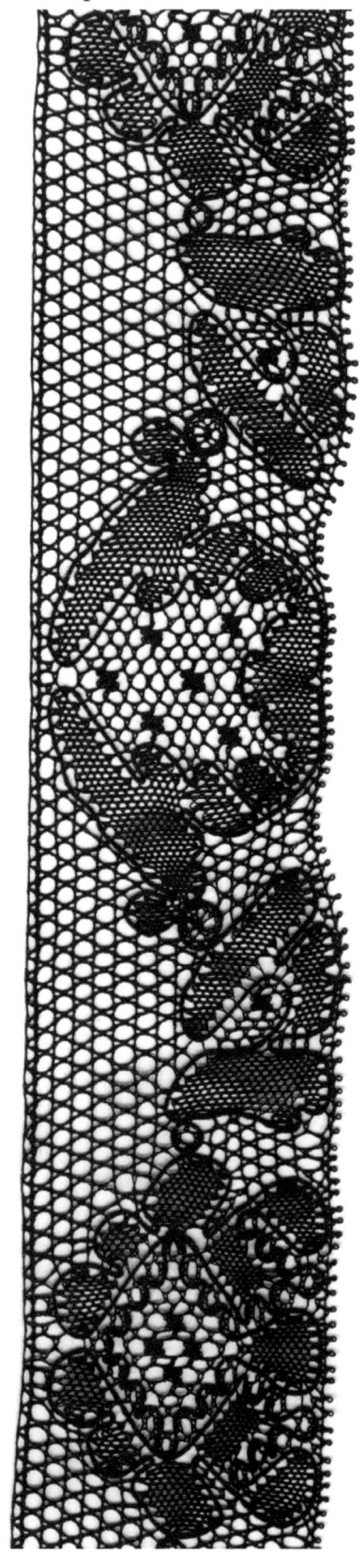

IPSWICH sample #22 made in Ipswich 1789-1790
Reconstructed sample by Karen H. Thompson, 2016
34 pairs + 1 pair gimp + 1 pair thin gimp thread or double thread for passive at foot side
For correct size, one repeat of the pricking is 22.1 cm or 8 11/16" long

See detailed diagrams on the following 2 pages

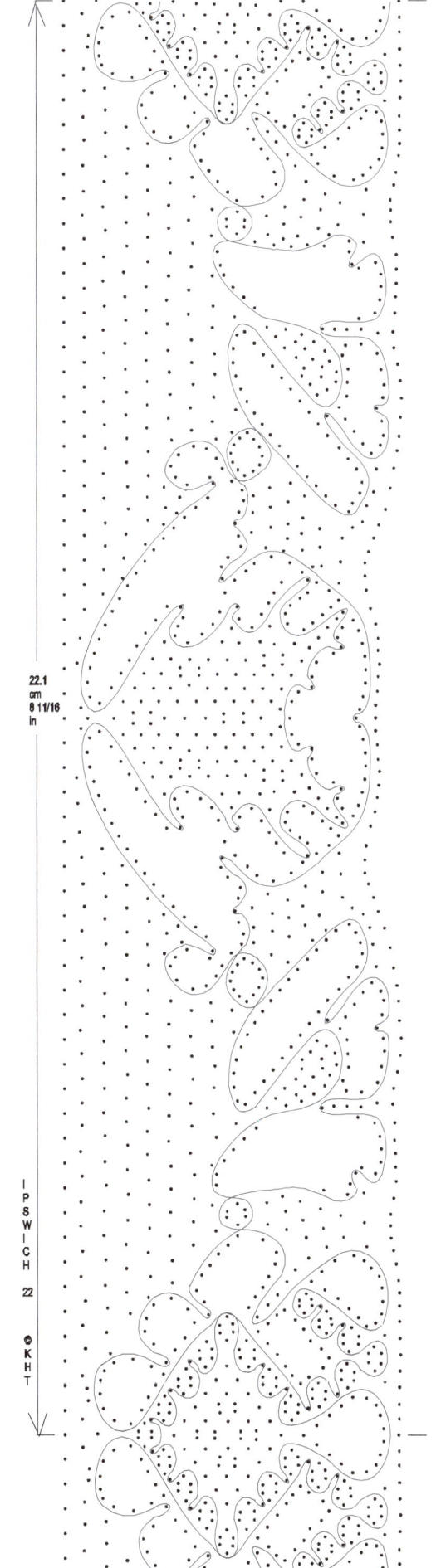

IPSWICH sample #22 made in Ipswich 1789-1790. Detailed working diagram p. 1

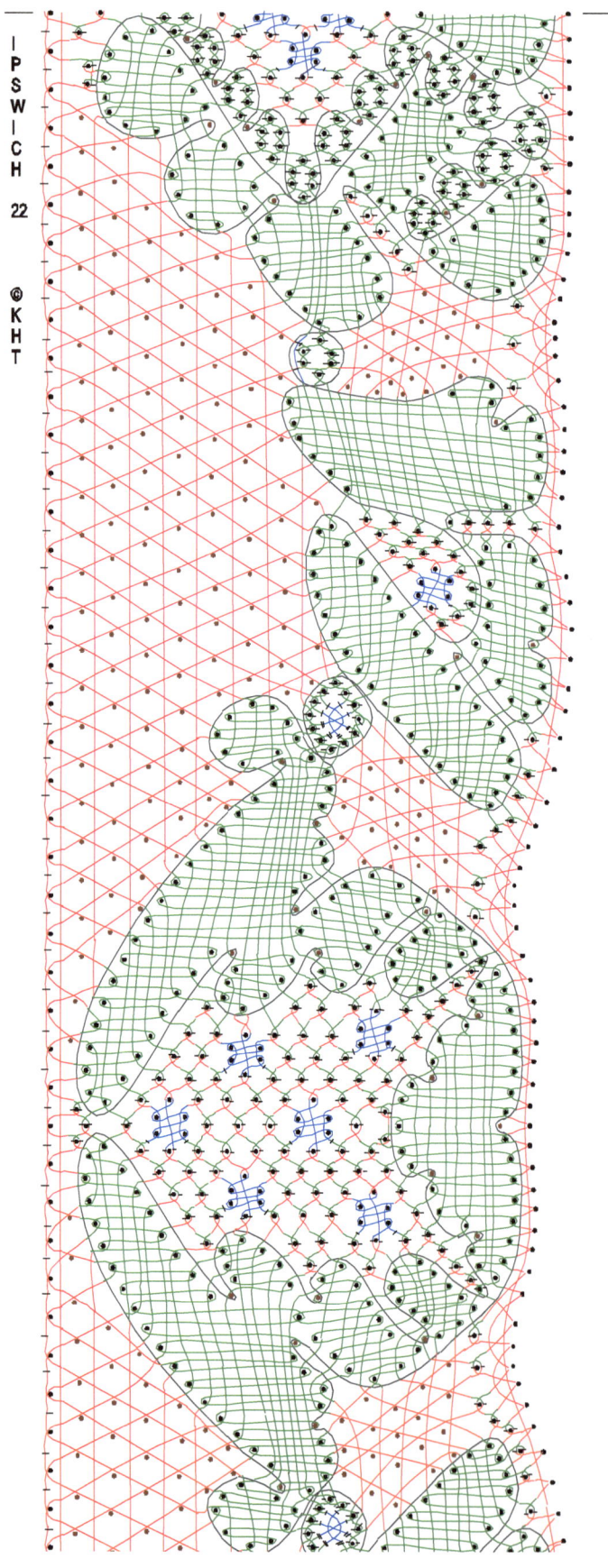

IPSWICH sample #22 made in Ipswich 1789-1790.

Detailed working diagram p. 2

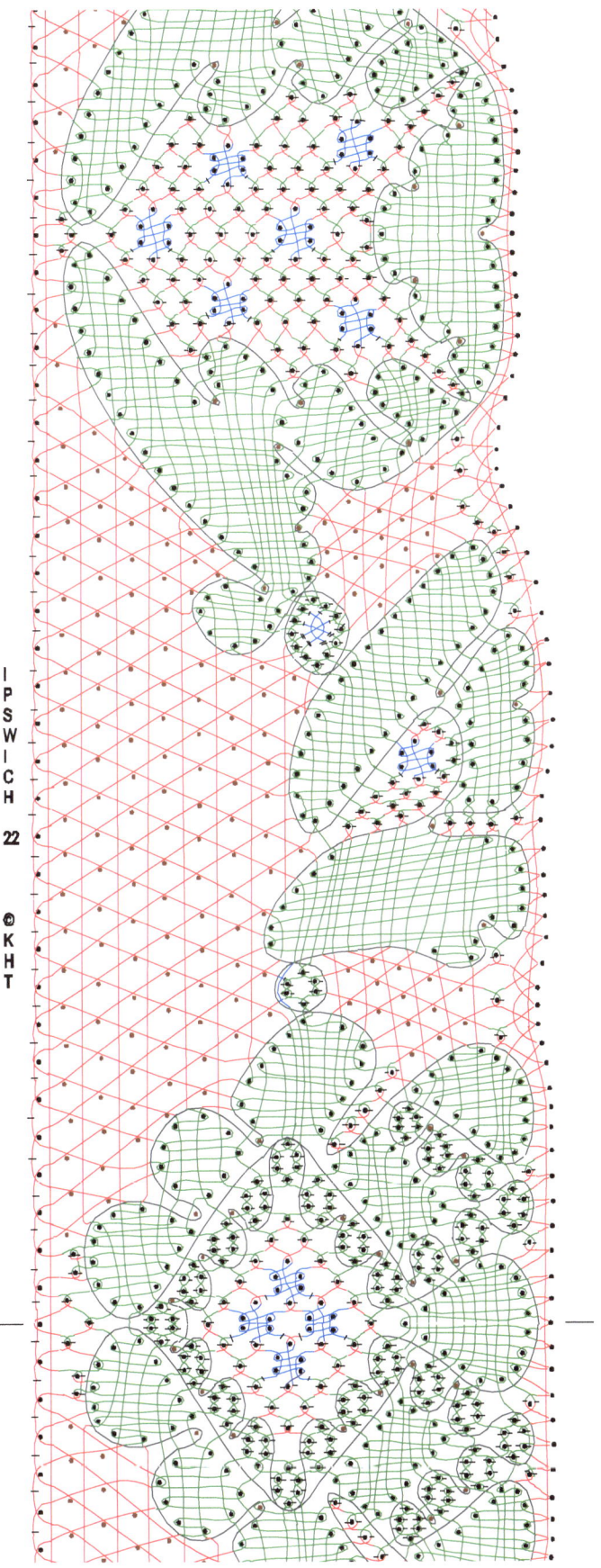

Karen H. Thompson

Contact: ipswichsamples@gmail.com

Karen Thompson grew up in Denmark and learned to make bobbin lace from her mother. That was more than 40 years ago, and since then she has taught many others how to make lace.
Specific to Ipswich Lace, Karen has reconstructed all 22 black silk lace samples that were sent to Secretary of Treasury Alexander Hamilton in 1790 from Ipswich, MA, as part of the first census of manufactures. One of her reconstructed Ipswich lace samples from 1789-1790 has been on public display in the "Within These Walls…" exhibit at the Smithsonian American History Museum since 2001.

Committed to education, Karen has attended lace conferences locally, nationally, and internationally, sometimes as a student, and just as often as a teacher or lecturer. Since the late 1990s, Karen has been working as a volunteer in Textiles with the lace collection at the Smithsonian Museum of American History. Her goal is to further the interest in historic lace, lace identification, lace making and to document as many of the laces in the collection as possible to make them available for online study.

Select print and web publications:

"Lacemaking in Ipswich, Massachusetts: An Unlikely Enterprise" Piece Work Magazine, May/June 2008. 36-41

"Ipswich Lace at the Smithsonian" OIDFA Bulletin 3, 2002, 24-27 (Quarterly Journal of the International Bobbin and Needle Lace Organization)

The Lace Collection at the Smithsonian Museum of American History:
http://americanhistory.si.edu/collections/object-groups/lace-collection

The World War One Laces at the Smithsonian:
http://americanhistory.si.edu/collections/object-groups/world-war-one-laces

"The delicate "war laces" of World War I" at the Smithsonian:
http://americanhistory.si.edu/blog/delicate-war-laces-world-war-i

"The finer details of the Hapsburg Imperial Bridal Veil" at the Smithsonian:
http://americanhistory.si.edu/blog/2011/06/the-finer-details-of-the-hapsburg-imperial-bridal-veil.html

"The Bayeux Tapestry at the Smithsonian? Yes, but who made it, when, where and why?"
http://americanhistory.si.edu/blog/2012/09/the-bayeux-tapestry-at-the-smithsonian-yes-but-who-made-it-when-where-and-why.html

"The Torchon Lace Company: The fine line between entrepreneurship and fraud" at the Smithsonian:
http://americanhistory.si.edu/blog/torchon-lace-company-fine-line-between-entrepreneurship-and-fraud

www.ingramcontent.com/pod-product-compliance
Lightning Source LLC
Chambersburg PA
CBHW041700160426
43191CB00002B/40